Broken Chains: A story of hope, healing & Freedom
Patrick "Doc" Nave

BROKEN CHAINS

First edition. June 19, 2024.

ISBN: 979-8227124487

Written by Patrick "Doc" Nave.

This book is dedicated to all those who went through the horror of being trafficked. I have never met such resilient people in my entire life and I am in awe of your determination to never give up.

"Will you accept the charges?"

The operator was on the other line and as I stood there with the telephone in hand, I could hear my father's voice in the background. I informed the operator that I would accept the charges, and I heard the click that signified she was now off the line.

My father spoke to me now without the filter of Bell Telephone and what he said to me would drain all emotion out of my life. "Son, you have to protect our home."

I knew what that meant because for the last couple of years my father had taught me what I was to do if things got out of hand, and he was unable to be there. I was to go into his bedroom, look under the bed and take out the guns that he had placed there. I was told to load them up, walk calmly into the living room, turn over the couch, squat behind it and watch the front door.

My father told me, "If the doorknob twitched at all just start firing." Afterwards, he told me, "When you are finished, take the guns, wipe off your fingerprints, and then go out the back door to the canal that ran behind the elementary school near to our house and drop the guns into the canal and RUN. Go as far away as you can, and call Paul who lives in North Carolina and he will come get you."

That was the plan and when my father spoke to me that evening, I knew it was up to me to protect my younger brothers and mother.

I know it seems strange hearing a tale like this, but my life was far from normal. My father had successfully risen in the ranks of the South Florida mob and, as a result, I had been introduced to various people of ability and talent. There was Mike, the jeweler who ran a diamond company that was funded by the mob. Mike had served time for a high-ranking mob official and, as a result, was given a wonderful company upon his release from prison. There was Bud, who became my godfather and who ran the mafia operations up to the Tennessee border. Bud lived in a townhome and ran pig farms to help launder his money. There was Stubs, a man who had gotten caught by the mob cheating and had his little pinky finger cut off as a reminder of what would happen to him if he ever chose to take that route again. Then there was Alfredo, the crazed Cuban who lived to party.

Alfredo hired me at the ripe old age of 14 to work at one of his furniture stores and later at an auto body shop in Miami, Florida. I delivered furniture with Rafael who was an explosives and weapons expert. One weekend when Alfredo was bored, he rented out part of a hotel on Miami Beach and we all partied and ate until we simply could not move. Alfredo was insane. He would have parties over at his house and light firecrackers and bottle rockets in the house, and you would have to keep on your toes so that you did not get into the line of fire. He was always going around with a Michelob beer in his hand, and you could tell from the tint of his eyes that he was probably on something else, as well.

There were a variety of colorful people in my life. The limping insurance guy who tried to have me killed, the politician who came over to convince my dad that he should fly down to Columbia and pick up yet another shipment of drugs, there was the crooked sheriff's deputy in Dade County who partied with my dad when it was convenient and, at times, when it was not.

So many people, all without morals, all intent on making money in an industry that was highly toxic and illegal.

If you have not guessed, my father was in the mafia—the mob—one of the cocaine cowboys of Miami, Florida fame and his nickname was "Peter Rabbit." I am not sure as to how he came about with the insignia, but it stuck to him and, as a result, he was simply a fairytale. I was intrigued by his power, afraid of his temper, and was introduced to a world that most people only faintly know about through books and television.

My father told me once that the only way someone could even begin to understand what his life was like was to watch the movie, "Scarface" with Al Pacino.

I, on the other hand, knew all too clearly what life in the mob was all about. We lived in a shroud of secrecy, drove cars that were stolen, kept the blinds shut because my father did not trust anyone, and never had a friend come into our home. We were raised in darkness and exposed to all sorts of abuse. Discipline involved my dad beating us with a horse whip when we were smaller, and then as we grew up it transformed into him throwing a knife at us, always missing of course, but sending the fear of death deep within our souls. We knew better than to disobey and so the seeds were planted deep within us so that if we stepped out of line we would be severely punished.

The night he asked me to defend our home, the FBI had arrested him. An Agent Donahue had left his business card on our dining room table, and my dad had informed me that some other people were going to try to harm our family. I followed his request and set the plan in motion. I moved the cars out into the darkness, grabbed my dad's sawed-off shotgun and a few other guns, and flipped the couch over and for hours kept my eyes peeled on the doorknob. If it had turned, I would have fired.

This book is an attempt to make an insane life make sense, an attempt to turn the scars of abuse and shame in my life into badges of God's glory. Clearly, Satan's plans to break me were powerful, but God intervened to strengthen me. I am not sure "WHY" He did so, I only know that He did. I should have been killed and yet no matter what transpired in my life God kept me going, building a resilient heart and soul.

I share part of my life with you because I want you to know that no matter what you have gone through or what you are going through, there is always hope.

Carlos Castaneda said it this way, "We either make ourselves miserable or we make ourselves strong. The amount of work is the same."

It is my prayer that each of us works on making ourselves strong. On embracing a positive view of the future.

Chapter One

With every story there is always a beginning, and my tale began with a less than spectacular start at St. Joseph's Hospital in Pontiac, Michigan on June 6, 1965. My mother would always tell me that I was supposed to be twin girls and for most of my life I took that to be a joke. However, as an adult I learned I was supposed to be a twin and the sister in the womb with me never made it out.

My entrance into this world served as the guide for which my life was to unfold. Lies, secrecy and darkness were to permeate my existence and even now I learn more about the so-called truth that had been covered up repeatedly almost on a daily basis. Not just from my own life but from the lies of a generational curse that followed my family for at least 100 years.

I entered the world like any innocent child but if I could have vetoed the choice of parents, I probably would have. Who wants to be born and live in the home of a drug dealer's family that covered up sexual crimes, greed, anger, murder, and many other issues? It sounds cool in the movies because a person can hide behind the television screen with their bucket of popcorn and watch the fiction unfold but to live it? That was not nearly as cool. It meant that every day of your life the hypervigilant state of your mind would be on high alert.

My father was the youngest of five and his parents were Nina and Mack Nave from Protem, Missouri. Protem was a little hamlet in southern Missouri that was near the border of Arkansas. My dad was the pup of the family, and he remembered growing up in the foothills of Missouri with great fondness. He would hunt all kinds of animals, swim with the snakes in the rivers and was content to just exist with nature. However, the world was a toxic place for my father and evil grew in his heart from an early age.

My grandfather, Mack, was a very mean and twisted man who had many brushes with the law and did not think twice about cheating on his wife. After a while, Mack was arrested and was on his way to serving time in prison when he escaped and for the rest of his life dodged the law until cancer caught up in Michigan, then finally the law caught up with him too.

Of course, I found out about my grandfather one day when I picked up a Leeper, Michigan newspaper and on the front page was the celebrated anniversary of when the dangerous outlaw, Mack Nave, was caught and arrested. I can remember thinking, "what?" I had no idea as to what my grandfather was capable of and since he had died before I was born, I had no memory of him either. All I had heard were stories of his craziness, but I just figured he was a rebel. Apparently, he was a rebel and a fugitive.

One of the favorite stories that got repeated about Mack was that as a young man his father offered him a hefty sum of money and a ranch in Missouri. Mack, being the carefree type of dude, turned down the offer as he did not want to be tied down and so he began to be a drifter, in and out of trouble, always carousing around looking for the next great adventure.

In hindsight, Mack was born in the wrong century. He needed to be living around the time of the Civil War when outlaws were rampant and the urge to head West filled many a young man with adventure and suspense. This urge for action, the unknown, for adventure is one of the curses that flows through the blood of the Nave clan. Never satisfied with the status quo, they are always striving, seeking for that next hit of adrenaline.

As a young boy, the years of living on the run took their toll on my dad. Dad had to live on the outskirts of the law and found himself settling down in a shed that he had turned into a small house, or a barn, or some other nondescript place where they could hide out. At one point, one of the insecure places he lived caught fire, and his few earthly possessions were burned up in a fire. His life was rotten, haggard, and poor. This type of existence birthed rage within him and his desire for wealth, to rise above the poverty level, was fanned into a consuming flame. As an adult, Dad was always trying to make a buck, improve his life, and make it to the "big time."

During his growing up years he only had one source of stability, his mom, my granny, Nina Maude Nave, quite possibly the toughest woman you could ever know. If you had ever watched the "Beverly Hillbillies" when it was on television, you would have seen a tough as nails Granny Clampett. Granny Nina was tougher still, a bit heavier, and a bit coarser. She carried a .38 pistol in her purse and had been known to brandish it when needed.

The memories of my Granny were quite colorful. She was our doctor, sage, and do it all person. When I needed a tooth pulled, she would call over to my Uncle Joe and he would hold me down and she would straddle me and take out her doctorin' tools, which in the case of tooth pullin' consisted of a set of vice-grips. She would latch onto the tooth and heave with all her might and the poor tooth never stood a chance. I learned early on never to complain about a loose tooth.

Of course, she was more than a dentist. In fourth grade I made the mistake of growing a seed wart on the bottom of my foot. Looking for some pity I complained and before I knew it my uncle had me pinned on the hood of her car and Granny had gotten out a knife and started doctorin' me right there on the spot. She dug into the seed wart determined to eradicate it from my foot. There was no pain reliever and if I complained my uncle was quick to challenge my manhood.

I kept telling him that even a man would at least get a bullet to bite down on. He was not impressed and just told me to suck it up.

I grew up thinking that my Granny had been a nurse, and it was not until after I had graduated college that I learned that Granny had simply worked as a custodian at a mental hospital, and it was while she was in that job that she acquired all her doctorin' skills. If I had known that at the time I would have been terrified of her but since I did not, I was always in awe of her surgical magic. I mean one time, my older brother split open his foot on a bottle in the lake and Granny was called to fix it up. I imagined that he was going to be taken to the hospital as there was blood flowing everywhere but not so. Granny got out her turpentine and rubbing alcohol and before we knew it, she had tied a rag around Jim's foot and the healing had commenced.

A few weeks later she had to try her healing methods on my knee as I had decided that I was Superman and had carefully placed a towel around my neck, securing it with a clothes pin, and had dashed down the hillside behind our house before launching myself into the air. I was certain that I could fly but at the ripe old age of five I learned suddenly that I could not. I landed on a stump that had an old rusty nail sticking out of it and it pretty much tore up my kneecap.

I was in agony, once again made the mistake of howling, and Granny was quick to the rescue. She cleaned out the wound, and for the rest of that summer I was placed on a lounge chair for my knee to heal, and the strangest part was that it healed. Of course, I have this nice little scar to show for it but in my mind the legend of Granny grew by leaps and bounds. I knew this little rotund lady could do anything.

My father learned the same things about his mom, my Granny, growing up as well. She proved to be the only stable thing in his life and every picture or story about Dad growing up involved some connection with Granny. She was ever present and served as the glue that held everything together.

Dad was the youngest of five kids and the influence of his father impacted them all. Dan was the oldest child, and he grew up wild as a buck. The Nave blood flowed recklessly through him, and Uncle Dan had a reputation as fearing nothing. He did anything and everything from riding wild horses in a rodeo to serving time in prison for other, more serious, crimes. He had a raging temper and was an alcoholic. By the time I met him he was living in our living room as he had gotten drunk one night and was involved in a car accident which had left him paralyzed.

He was in an old hospital bed that we had to wind up and down. It was in the 1970's so there were no cool gadgets to help him, so he just laid in that bed. He would ask us to move him over or turn the tv on or get him a book from time to time but he was really hampered by his health. He could move his shoulders and elbows, but his hands were fused almost like a "C." He could turn his neck, but the rest of his body did not cooperate. As he got older, he grew calmer and by the time I was in high school he was this wise sage that offered advice and tried to guide me, tried. If only I had listened.

Granny became his nurse, which also fostered the faulty concept that she was some amazing miracle medical worker.

The next two kids that Granny had were girls, Aunt Wanda, and Aunt Betty. Aunt Wanda married a guy whose family owned a small equivalent of a Home Depot, called Pontiac Plywood. Her family did well and soon they were living on 20 acres with lots of money but as she grew wealthier, she grew more conceited and eventually alienated her entire family. Aunt Betty, however, was the person most closely resembled Granny. She was loving, caring and tried her best to stay connected with our family.

But then there was Uncle Joe. Uncle Joe was nine years older than my father and stepped in when Dad was arrested. He was about the same height and build and had the same temperament to boot. The Nave "reaction" or curse was prevalent with him as well. One of the first stories I heard about Uncle Joe was the time he was walking down the street with Aunt Mona, his wife. Some guy made a lewd remark about Aunt Mona and then kept on driving.

Uncle Joe noticed that the dude got stopped at a red light and so he ran after the guy, who when he saw Uncle Joe, rolled up his window in fear. Not to be outdone, Uncle Joe let his rage take care of business and punched the guy through the window. The sacrifice of his hand was of no consequence when it came to appeasing Uncle Joe's anger.

Once at Uncle Joe's house he told me that eventually there came a time when he knew that he was faced with a crossroad. Either he was going to follow the downward trail of the typical Nave, or he was going to have to fight to change. He was determined to fight for a different existence and so he turned away from the typical Nave trajectory and ended up avoiding the criminal way of life. He went to work for GMC and started buying and selling old houses. He showed me how it was possible to escape the criminal way but to be honest with you, it seemed incredibly boring. The price for stability? Was it worth it?

Chapter Two

Granny was the safe haven for my father and so as peas in a pod my dad and granny grew up together. Dad had experienced a great deal of personal loss in his life and when his few possessions had been burned up, he was changed. As a result, he was determined to make a difference in this life. He worked odd jobs, kept tight to the side of my grandmother, and his early teen years found him going around as the perfect rebel, complete with the collar up on his leather jacket. In my mind I had him pegged as a rebellious Fonzie, from Happy Days, but he leaned more towards the Marlon Brando image.

He was cool, tough, and adorned with an attitude that dripped off him. He met my teenage mother around this time who was also having a tough go of it in life. Joyce, my mother, was the product of divorce. She was living with her mother, had an older stepsister and a younger baby brother. She bounced around from home to home as her mom moved and at one point her stepfather did not want anything to do with her. It was that neglect that made her the perfect vulnerable target and my cool dad swept in to rescue her.

It was the love she was looking for and so she started hanging out with the tough guy, feeling protected and knowing in her heart that this rebel would take care of her and help her escape from her rotten stepfather. Their love grew and eventually they determined to seek out a life of their own. Of course, by the time that my mom's father found out about her rebel boyfriend he was about to go insane. He was the owner of a gas station in Peoria, a man of hard work and high ethics and he could see through the veneer of my dad and knew that he was a bad seed.

He did his best to tear apart the relationship that my father and mother had developed but the more he tried to rip it to shreds the firmer and more resolved their determination to stay together became.

Eventually, his desire to separate them lit a match of desperation and my mom, dad, and their trusty side kick, Granny, all took off and hid out in a gravel pit north of Detroit. They all lived in the equivalent of a shack and Granny, the do it all person, managed to forge a birth certificate for my mother and so somewhere around the age of 16 or 17, my dad and mom got legally or should I say, illegally, hitched.

Not too long after their marriage my mom got pregnant and the idea of the "Leave it to Beaver" family was hatched and there was high hope for my mom that she had finally found her dream and my dad had finally gotten his family and Granny, well, she just became a mom to another child and was soon to take on a caregiver role for my older brother as well.

During this time, my dad convinced my grandmother to purchase a gas station with him in Pontiac. She never really could say no to my dad and as a result the gas station was purchased, and Dad was officially on his way to earning that fortune that had always alluded him.

The Station did not work out as he had hoped so they had to sell the station and Dad, against his entrepreneurial nature, went to work doing this and that until he finally got a good job at the automotive factory in town. During the 60's working for one of the big three automakers was everyone's dream. Southeastern Michigan was the home of General Motors, which made Pontiac, Chevrolet, and GMC. It was also the home of Chrysler/Dodge and Ford as well. The big three automakers provided good wages and a healthy future and so my dad signed on at GMC and went to work in the paint department. Dad wanted to be on his own, but he needed to make sure that he had some source of income. He reluctantly traded in his life, or so he thought, and accepted the monotonous job of factory worker.

His job was to climb a ladder and paint the hard-to-reach areas of the larger vehicles that were produced at the factory. It was a respectable job, a steady job, but it lacked what every Nave needed. Spice! The mundane task of going to work every day, of being a regular "joe," of being stuck in a plant chafed my dad and he constantly found himself thinking about how to break out of the rut. This disease of will has impacted each one of the members of my family line and it continues to do so even today.

Eventually, he settled on the perfect plan for wealth development and when he was up on a ladder painting an oversized truck, he conveniently lost his footing and fell off the ladder landing him under a doctor's care and a lawsuit quickly followed. There might have been a suspicion that my dad had deliberately thrown himself off that ladder, but nothing could be proven so a judgment was reached, and my dad received a large pay off, with which he used to seed his potential empire.

He purchased an apartment complex in Pontiac, Michigan and set about becoming a Real Estate Tycoon.

My oldest brother, Jimmy, was born around this time in 1961 and he brought immense joy to my parents, but their lives were balancing on the edge of a volcano. The hopeful relationship that my mom had dreamed of proved to be more fiction than fact and the moment that my mom and dad ran off together, even though Jimmy was born, she could sense the evil side of my dad.

She dug in and did her best to protect my brother, but the Nave disease was rampant in my dad, and she knew that she had to escape. Dad was out like a dog in heat, looking for any woman who would hook up with him, and his idea of faithfulness was that mom would always be there for him and that she would be faithful but that there was a whole separate set of rules for him. He was the angry man, the driven one, the one full of potential but my mom saw him as a person that would ruin her life.

She did the only thing she could. She ran off with Jimmy with the help of her father who had always been against my dad. She disappeared and my grandfather, Irv, hid them out. It would have been a wonderful escape, but my father was not one to give up easily. He got together with my Granny, and they went to see a fortune teller. The fortune teller told my dad where Jimmy was being held and so my dad and his accomplice, Granny, drove down to Kansas and proceeded to kidnap my brother without the knowledge of my mother.

After getting Jimmy into their car, they started driving off right at the moment my mother made the discovery that he was missing. She ran outside just in time to see them driving away and my dad yelled out to her, "If you want to see your son you had better get in the car." That day marked the beginning of the end for my mother. She made the only decision she could. She would give everything up for the sake of her kid. That momentous decision followed her as she eventually had three other boys. No matter what my father dragged her into she could not let go of him, it was an addiction of sorts, and she could not run off because she would never abandon her children.

Mixed into this tale, was my dad's distorted religious beliefs. Even though he was a rebel, deep down inside he craved a relationship with God. My granny had been exposed to the truth of Jesus Christ through the tireless work of a literature evangelist who came knocking on her door. She somehow scraped up enough money to buy a set of religious books that had been published by the

Seventh-day Adventist Church and as a result, she became an early convert to the Seventh-day Adventist movement.

Granny resolved to raise her family up with God and so her five kids were all exposed to the Adventist church and three out of the five ended up joining, my dad being one of the three. He read the Bible, went through times of great faith, and then would have times of greater rebellion. Years ago, there was a country music song by the group Forerunner which had in the lyrics, "half of my blood is Cain's blood, half of my blood is Abel's." Nothing could be truer of my dad. He seemed to bounce back and forth from Cain to Abel, always fighting against himself.

Chapter Three

My mom and dad got married, somehow survived the turbulent early years, and when I was born in 1965 my uncle helped my father buy his first home. With the money that my dad got from GMC, he began to build his empire and purchased an apartment complex and my only memory of that complex involved one night when dad drove me to the apartment complex amidst gunfire and told me to stay down. He then ran off and left me at the ripe old age of four and I had no idea what was going on but stayed low and prayed that any stray bullets would miss me. As you can imagine, the stress of that time was indicative of what life was like living in the Nave household.

I had to stay hidden behind this hedge and with my head tucked low I kept hearing gunshots off in the distance and I did not know if my father was dead or alive. He was like John Wick in my mind, always capable of getting out of any trouble and when I saw him race into the distance, I was both terrified and proud.

The result of such a life was that as a small child I developed nervous tics. Some thought I had Tourette Syndrome, where one's neurological system was overwhelmed, and you could not resist the buildup of neurological energy. The incredible tension was so high that my dad's family doctor said that he had never seen a family like ours. He said if it were up to him, he would "medicate the whole bunch."

I have since learned that there are five levels of trauma response that we each potentially can experience. The first level is white and if you are living on that level nothing bad has really happened to you. Life has been easy, safe, and your family of origin is a place of comfort and healing. If your experience is level white, then each day you would wake up calm and relaxed. The Vegus nerve that runs from the Brain Stem to your stomach would be sending "calm" signals and your bowels, stomach and head would all be near the state known as homeostasis or chill.

But if you had experienced a small amount of negativity. Some things had happened in your past, but you still had a strong, healthy family to support you and were able to go through whatever took place and heal, then you would be someone who would be living life on level, "yellow." Yellow meant that when you woke up each day, there might be a little uneasiness, but you were hopeful and optimistic. It was a fairly good place to be.

The next level is Orange. You are in Orange if you have had some negative things happen in your life and know they will happen again. You do not know when, so your inner radar is on high alert constantly scanning for threats. It takes a lot of mental energy at this level and if you are an Orange person your stomach and bowels will usually have some stress related issues. On a good day I am Orange and sometimes I even make it to the next level, Red.

Red is when you have had some trauma in your life, and you know it is going to happen and you have identified what the threat is. It could be an appointment, meeting someone, a trigger or anything. Red is that state where you have identified the threat, and your stress hormones are flooding your body in anticipation because you know you must deal with the threat.

The final level is Black. Black is where the threat is so bad, and you cannot escape it, so you simply enter a state of automatic function and you black out until it is over. For some this might involve disassociating but for others it will involve utilizing that fight, flight or freeze instinct that kicks in with our parasympathetic or sympathetic nervous systems.

When I was molested and/or trafficked, I would disassociate, as that would allow me to place my mind in a better place while negative things were happening to my body. It also caused my mind to develop this filter of constantly searching out for the negative. It was hard to shut down and just "be." I always expected the next worse thing to occur.

When I was a child, my experience ranged from orange to black. Thus, the nervous tics from the trauma.

During my early years, my dad started to expand his fortune and went into business with my Uncle Joe in a corvette restoration shop. He would buy wrecked Corvette's, fix them up and sell them for a profit. Also, during this time my one good childhood memory emerged. My dad bought a huge old bus, painted it green and we spent about a month touring from Michigan to Missouri riding in that big green bus. That is why one of my favorite movies today is the movie, "RV," with Robin Williams because he rented a big green RV and toured with the family. And yes, I do know that it is a cheesy movie, but I like it none the less.

It did not take long for my dad and uncle to disagree about the Corvette Shop. One day, a few years ago, my uncle told me that the reason the shop did not work out was because dad was always trying to rip him off financially and eventually Uncle Joe could not take it. My Uncle was doing all the work, and my dad would conveniently find ways to hang out with people who were using drugs or getting wasted in life. He wanted to appear like he was king of the hill so my uncle would work, and my dad would spend. They went their separate ways and dad was on to other things to build his fortune.

He would buy a house or a car, fix it up, and then sell it for a profit. We would live in the house for a brief time and then when the house was ready, we would move. We bounced around and it is hard to remember all the houses that came and went. My dad would do whatever it took to make money and it seemed that whatever he touched profited, but it could never satisfy the innate desire that he had to make more. He bought an 80-acre farm in Ortonville, Michigan and a 300-acre ranch in Eldon, Missouri. Pretty soon his third child was born, Todd, and we seemed like the perfect little family.

I can remember time after time being complemented by people in church, yes, through it all we still were faithful attenders at a local church, as to how well behaved we were and how handsome we looked but no one had a clue as to what was really going on. We were the perfect illusion of what a godly family should look like, and I can remember one picture of that time where we were all dressed up in our living room getting ready for church. My dad had conquered the outward illusion but inside our family was a seething cauldron of dysfunction. My dad had a raging temper and a bit of a control problem to boot. Early on he would discipline us with a horse whip. He would strike out at our bare skin, and we would have welts, cuts, and bruises. If we ever touched someone else's vehicle, we would be whipped with a belt. We were taught to respect everyone and if we ever showed any disrespect we would be punished. Now, disrespect was defined by my father's mood, so it was a thing that was not really defined. You could get beat for talking back, laughing at the dinner table, being a minute late for some appointment, or for any reason that seemed remotely feasible at the moment.

We would sit at the dinner table, and no one would breathe until we knew what type of mood dad was in. He had these ice blue eyes, and you could never tell whether he was aggravated or in a good state of mind and you did not want to stir him up if he was in anything less than a positive mind set. We walked on eggshells as he was always on the cusp of exploding.

I can remember having to sit perfectly still in church. If we giggled or got out of control we were pinched by my mother or given the death stare by my father. It always seemed that when we got home from church we were spanked because we just could not behave. I can remember one stretch of time where we would come home from church, and I would run to my room and kneel on my bed to pray because I knew that my father would not spank me if I was praying. That tactic only worked for so long, however, and soon even prayer did not stop the wrath from being dished out.

But as bad as my dad's behavior was, another thing slipped into our home that was even worse. By the age of three I had been sexually molested and for years I went through being abused by various people who had access to our home. I was so starved for love that anyone that wanted to hold me was rewarded with whatever behavior they requested. Another terrible thing that my father tried to do was to create a sense of racial prejudice. My father used to brag that he was part of the Klu Klux Klan, I am not sure if he ever was or not, but I do know that he gave me a medallion one day that had KKK on it and threatened me that if I ever had a black friend or tried to date a black girl that he would kill me.

To this day I am grateful that God did not allow any racial prejudice to develop in my mind. It appears whatever my dad meant for evil, God in some miraculous way, turned to good. I wish the trauma did not impact as much either, but unfortunately, the trauma imprinted upon my brain still raises its ugly head sometimes.

As I write the updated version of this book, which has taken me years to put down on paper because I did not want to acknowledge all the crap that happened in my life, I write it with mixed emotions. If you have ever been abused, you know the reality of that pain and the guilt and shame that accompany it. I still struggle with the effects of those years and time after time I see little kids and imagine how sick someone had to be to abuse a child. It is one of the driving reasons why my wife and I started Bikers Against Trafficking in 2016 which fights to eliminate human sex trafficking.

By the age of 5 I knew a great deal about sex. I had been taught by that ripe old age to disassociate what happened to me from who I was. My body was physically and sexually abused but I refused to let my mind accept it. I have more memories with my clothes off than with them on during this time and as a result I developed a false sense of sexuality. It was something "dirty" and to be "ashamed of," yet at the same time something I yearned for and wanted.

The confusion between good and bad was imprinted in my brain and you have to imagine that as one grows older and hits the teenage years and later, sexuality was one big mess. The question kept permeating my brain, "Why did I want something that was so bad?" "Why did I seemingly enjoy being molested?"

Of course, when you are a child, your logic is faulty and so a lot of times, we simply think everything that happens was our fault. The tainted view of sexuality was one that was pressed deep within my psyche and takes a therapeutic journey to heal from it on any level or to any degree.

All I wanted was for someone to accept and love me. For my father, especially, to be proud of me but he was too busy with everyone else and eventually it all came to a head, because in the Spring of 1974, I went to bed one night and woke up the next morning and my father was gone.

Chapter Four

The night my father disappeared was a night like most others. At some point during the evening, we would have been told to do our chores and at the age of eight my big chore was the nightly dishes, which I hated. I am sure I went to the sink with something less than a positive attitude and I am sure this might be one of the reasons my father was upset with me that particular night. But whatever really happened, one thing I know for sure. I went to bed that night determined to make a point and so I did not tell my dad good night, which had been my ritual, and as a result there was no good night kiss and hug. I simply trotted up the stairs and into my little hall closet that had been turned into a bedroom and shut the door.

The next morning my anger had subsided, and I went to seek him out only to discover that somehow in the night, he had disappeared, and I had no idea where he had gone. My eight-year-old mind immediately started to process this information and the conclusion that my logic came to was that my father had run away from home because he was mad at me. I knew the tactic of running away because between the years of three and five, I tried to run away from home multiple times.

The first time I simply packed up a few belongings and tied them on a stick like a hobo and took off walking. I had no idea where I was going but I was leaving behind the home where I had been abused. I walked until it turned dark and then as I tried to figure out how I was going to survive, I heard my name called and knew that I should go back. Another time, I climbed a big tree up near my Granny's house and with a few items in a pillowcase I was going to live in that tree forever.

I could hear everyone calling out my name, but I was not coming out. The idea of living in a tree, where I was safe, appealed to me and so I stayed until I ran out of food and once again my little four-year-old logic betrayed me because I finally gave in and surrendered.

I thought it was my fault because the night he ran off and disappeared I went to bed without giving him a kiss and a hug because I was mad at him. Now he was gone, he had disappeared, and I was racked with guilt.

No one spoke of his whereabouts for months and the tension in our home was very high. We were living on 80 acres in Ortonville, Michigan at the time and my mind went through all the scenarios as to why my dad would leave me. Even though my grandmother and uncle lived with us during this time of uncertainty the ache grew daily.

Four months later my cousin secretly told me that my dad had been arrested and that put me into shock. My dad had been arrested on charges of First-degree murder and was accused of killing two men in a drug deal that had gone sour up near Port Huron, Michigan. I never believed that my dad could have ever done something that horrible and I can remember sitting behind him in the courtroom trying to understand how anyone could think that he had done anything wrong.

As word leaked out that my dad had been arrested and charged with murder it was beyond my wildest imagination. I had just turned nine and in my world things like "this" did not happen. My dad was toxic, abusive, and dangerous but in my little boy's head I still wanted him more than any other person in my life. I had convinced myself that if I were just 'good enough' he would be proud of me and would not have to hurt me. My wife likes to say, "The hell we live is better than the hell we don't know."

I knew the hell of living with my father, but I also believed at that time that every kid went through something similar. The idea that kids were to be silent around adults; do whatever they were told; were abused and molested; beaten with a horse whip; had knives thrown at them; etc... I had no concept that I had been molested, abused, and trafficked.

I felt as though I needed to do whatever it took to get my dad back home.

The first chance we got to see my dad, he was in jail in Port Huron, Michigan. The jail was a several hour car ride away from our home in Ortonville and when we got there, we were greeted by this huge building which touched the sky. It was the county jail and it looked like it was so tall that it would never end. Mom told us that we were going to go inside and visit and that is what we did. We went through those glass doors and entered a world of punishment. Bars, loud clanging noises, armed guards behind walls of glass.

We were left in the visitor seats while my mom went in for a visit and all around us were those who were in a similar situation. People who had a loved one in jail for whatever reason and what bonded us all together was our fierce determination that our loved ones were innocent, had gotten the shaft.

The visit went on for a while and we had to sit still, which you can bet we did. We did not know if the people around us were going to molest or kill us. We had been taught as young kids that police officers were bad, and they were everywhere. If the criminals did not get you then the corrupt law enforcement was going to use, you. Nowhere was safe and so the ever-vigilant warning system in my head was on full RED alert.

As we were leaving the jail that day my mom had us look up at a row of cells. She said there was one particular cell where my father was looking out at us and so he could see us. She had us look to see him waving but it was all a lie. I believed her at the time, no matter that the logic in my head said there was no way he could get back up and spot us like ants on the ground. I wanted to believe he was there, I needed to believe he was there but unfortunately, what did happen that day was the lies of the Nave clan grew further down into my crooked and hurting soul. My mother and other adults in our lives often lied to us in hopes that it made us feel better but in reality, it simply taught us not to trust anyone.

As the court proceedings dragged on, all our money went to lawyers, and we ended up broke and our farm in Ortonville started to become a dangerous place to be. People were out looking for my dad and so my Uncle Joe installed a gate, put up razor wire fencing and tried to do some things to discourage others from getting too close. The problem was that we were way out in the country with no one around and this was before security cameras, cell phones and the internet. Our greatest security tool was to hide when people pulled up to look for us.

It was eventually settled that we would have to leave our home and disappear. The place selected was the home of my Aunt Betty so one night we just snuck off, left the farm alone and disappeared into my aunt's spare bedroom. We were enrolled in a private school that was an hour away and were driven there daily and it seemed as if my family's plan was to survive whatever threat that was ongoing.

With all of our funds gone because of the lawyers, our father unable to work as he was in jail and my mom having to take care of four boys ages 13, 9, 7 and 1, life was chaotic, and we were helpless, homeless and full of fear.

We had lost our home and were now all crowded into a small bedroom unsure as to what was going on. We ended up on welfare and each time we had to go to the store to pay for our food with coupons from a booklet I felt as if everyone in the store was looking at me and talking about 'that poor little kid.' It seemed that whenever we had to go to the store that I drew the short stick and so I would grab the hated coupon book and make the trek up the long desolate sidewalk into the grocery store. I hated being poor, having a dad in jail, having to rely on others, and watching my mom in her agony.

I eventually learned what my dad had really done when I was searching his name on Google and found an article about him that was written by the then, Prosecuting Attorney in St. Clair County. Here is a synopsis: My father and two friends decided that they would drive to Port Huron, Michigan where this drug house was located out in the country. Their plan was to buy drugs from the two people that they were going to meet at the house and then after they had started the negotiation period to buy the drugs would pull out guns and simply steal the drugs.

The drug dealers reacted when told that my dad and his two associates were going to steal their drugs and so they pulled out guns and a gun battle ensued. One of my dad's friends was seriously wounded and the two drug dealers were captured where my father executed them after having them kneel before him and shooting them in the back of the head. It was a ruthless killing and then my father and colleagues set the house on fire as a way of burning up all the evidence.

The one friend that had been shot had gotten out of the house and crawled through the crops in the field to hide. It seems as though my dad and the one remaining associate were going to put their friend in the house to burn up as well but eventually, they simply left him in the field as they thought he was dead.

My father then left thinking that all the evidence had been burned up. However, when the fire trucks arrived after everyone had left, the man who had crawled into the field, an outlaw biker named Jesus, was still alive and he ended up recovering so that he could tell the police about the others. What my father thought had been the perfect crime ended up leaving evidence that built a path to his front door. Months after the crime, my father was arrested and charged with First Degree Murder.

During the court proceedings leading up to the trial we were brought into court every chance we could. My father's defense attorney, Mr. Fink, was intent on building sympathy with the judge and prosecutor and later the potential jurors. We were marched out, forced to sit on hard wooden benches behind my dad, and as everyone stared at us, we felt as though we were the objects of pity. It was good to see my father, but he looked and acted very differently, even going as far as to have lifts installed in his shoes so that he would appear taller in court.

On the day the trial was to begin my dad and the other man who had committed this crime took a plea deal and pled guilty to Second Degree murder and my father was given a sentence of 10-20 years.

He was sent away to the Jackson State Penitentiary in Jackson, Michigan and our life fully went into a free fall at that time. We began the humiliating, weekly ritual of driving from Pontiac to Jackson, Michigan. I can still retrace the steps in my mind. We would get on the interstate, drive by Ann Arbor where I would imagine one day I would attend the University of Michigan, and then head off onto the Jackson, Michigan exit. Signs were posted all along the highway warning people to avoid hitchhikers because a prison was located close by.

We would drive through the worst part of the city and on the horizon this huge red brick building would eventually emerge. It was surrounded by a high fence, rolls of razor wire were on top and near the bottom. Large guard towers were up high into the sky, and as we drove up to the entrance, we were stopped by armed employees of the prison. We were asked why we were there, and we would have to recite my father's prison number, which was 141154, a number that still rots in my brain to this very moment.

We would be allowed in and would find a parking space. We would then walk up to the large prison doors along with other people and once we entered the prison it was raw chaos. Hundreds of people were loitering. Small kids were jumping and running out of control, babies were screaming, vending machines lined the walls, rigid plastic chairs with multi-colored gum stuck to them dotted the landscape and on the far side was a place to check in and a wall of lockers.

We were given this key with a large silver metal piece attached. We were told all our belongings were to go into that locker, as we could not bring anything into the prison visiting room. We obeyed and began the wait that often-lasted hours for our small visit with our dad. Eventually, when our name was called, we lined up and like sheep led to the slaughter were ushered through the metal detector where we were searched, which felt like a rape. All honor and dignity were tossed out of the window and fear spun uncontrolled in our guts. Then the first set of iron bars were opened, and we stepped in, and they closed behind us.

Now we were trapped. Even though we had done nothing wrong, we were being treated as felons as well. Bars behind us and bars ahead of us. There was a large room off to the side behind glass where armed guards grimaced and stared at us. We slowly walked past a guard that was sitting down who took what looked like a huge Q-Tip and dipped it into some clear liquid and then made a huge cold mark on the backside of our hands. This was important because when we came out, we were forced to put that hand under an ultraviolet light and if a purple mark did not show up, we would not be allowed to leave.

Once I got that mark, I was terrified that somehow it would wipe off and I would be stuck for the rest of my life behind bars. It did not register in my little brain that they would be able to tell I was a kid, I thought that if anything happened, I would not be leaving. Eventually another set of bars would be opened, we would walk through and then a big steel door opened and we were herded into the large visiting room where there were cameras and guards everywhere. There were semi-circle arrangements of chairs spread out and we were told, warned, to behave.

We would find a place to squeeze in and then another door would buzz, and our dad would walk in and then he would smile at us and walk over. We had to be careful of any fast movements so we could not attack him with hugs but could only do the slow quiet hugs. He would then sit down with us, and we would take turns sitting next to him. We could feel the stares of the others, of the guards, of the cameras and my blood pressure always neared record highs. It was another RED level of stress.

The entire process was designed to strip all humanity from the person visiting and it seemed as though we were the guilty ones. The prison visiting experience combined with being on welfare and a history of abuse slowly weaved together and a hatred, a venom started to develop within me, and it would brew for a few more years until one day it exploded.

My older brother described one aspect of what happened to us during those days. The understanding of who the good guy was got distorted and we started seeing the police as the bad guys and the criminals as the innocent victims. The very people designated to assist, law enforcement, were painted as evil, not to be trusted.

We would look at the other inmates and their families and would feel a common bond. We were all in this together. The years of abuse were overlooked during this time because it had been drilled into our heads that when the world turned against us, we had to saddle up and defend ourselves from the evil "out there." No matter that the real evil was all around us at home, it seemed as though it was the cool thing to do to fight others. It also allowed more people to molest us because this sick, twisted way of justifying torture was unbelievable but all too real.

Chapter Five

We were attending a church in Holly, Michigan at the time and as things escalated and we became more destitute, the church stepped in to help us. Somehow, they got their hands on an old house in Holly, Michigan and offered us a great deal on renting it. We moved in and were provided for by that church. The poison in my soul ached and it was during this time that I determined to get my innocent dad out of prison.

I wrote President Jimmy Carter telling him that my dad was an innocent man and begged him to intervene in the case. I never heard back but that did not stop me. I wrote to the governor, as a matter of fact, my mom also tried to intervene in the government, but no one wanted to hear our cries of innocence, probably because my dad had plead guilty, but I had no idea that he had admitted to the crime.

It was during our time in Holly that several good things happened along with more, if you could believe it, tragedy as well. Several godly men from that church started to take an interest in us helping to fill the void that was deep within us. Mr. Chamberlain, a retired man from the church, became the caretaker of the property and he was like a grandfather to us. He was always coming around, fixing something, and encouraging us as best he could. Rick Sutton was another man who impacted our lives. Rick ran a local gas station and somehow befriended us along with the rest of his family and he served as a father figure to four small boys and used to wrestle with us on many occasions. The pastor of that church was incredible as well. His name was Earl Zager and he tried to pour into us God's love. I cannot say that they did not try but the evil side was pushing forward all the same.

The years we spent in Holly were ones where we got to see the good of what a church could do and yet we also saw the evil that church people could do as well. The sexual abuse continued in my life plus my Christian classmates teased me mercilessly for having a father in prison. Many times, I would be walking home from school with kids on the other side of the street screaming at me for being a loser for having a dad in prison. Once again, even though I had not done anything wrong, I felt as though I was the one being punished. I felt like I was evil and damned. The psychological damage of thinking that it was all YOUR fault sunk deep into the crevices of the brain and the little critic that resides there would often remind me that I was worthless, I was garbage and that I had no value.

I tried to escape by smoking cigarettes and drinking any alcohol I could get my hands on. There was this wooded area near our house, and I would go to Freeman's supermarket, steal a pack of cigarettes, and hide in the woods. I had seen on television that if you smoked cigarettes, you were cool and hip. I idolized the Marlboro man and I wanted to be like those cool, shade wearing people who smoked "Kool's." Unfortunately, the ones that were near the register where I could steal them were those long woman cigarettes, "Virginia Slims." I would grab a pack of them and then head out to the woods and just ignore the fact that they were girl cigarettes.

There were other kids out in the woods as well. Some of them had the cigarettes that I craved, Marlboro, so we would trade and at that moment I was free. I would put the cigarette up on my lips, light it with some matches and take that first drag. I was cool, I was hip, but I knew that deep down within my soul the ache was still there. I wanted more than anything to escape the life I was living.

I tried working to make money. I got a paper route, actually two. I sold Tupperware, tried to wheel, and deal Avon and I would use whatever money I got for my mom. The seeds of "taking care of everyone" and becoming the perfect co-dependent person were planted deep and I started making sure that I was in charge as the caretaker. In some small way it made me feel appreciated and even though my body was being molested, my brain somehow found value in keeping things tidy. In paying the bills, in taking care of others. I knew that I had to pay the price of abuse, but I was hoping that by paying it myself, others could escape the terror.

We had no money and at Christmas there were usually a few people in the church giving us leftover stuff or things that were clearly found at the Salvation Army. We were the kids that were invisible, that no one wanted, that had no worth, that Santa forgot about. I hated holidays because I hated the models, broken toys, and other things that well intentioned church people brought to us.

They never wrapped the presents. They were just there in all their simplicity serving as a reminder that we were not important.

Developmental Psychologists tell us that those first few years of life are important in our development. One of the first things we learn is whether the world is a safe place or not. The first couple years of life the small child would read the adults in their life and determine, by the adults' reactions and behavior, whether the world was safe. My world was sexual abuse, getting beat, yelled at, and when I was in the womb, my mom fell several flights of stairs. I think it would be a good guess that my mind rapidly determined that the world was NOT a safe place.

The second big lesson is whether we are unconditionally loved or not. I knew as a small child that I was to be seen and not heard. When there were family dinners, I was always placed at the small kids' table, we were told to keep it quiet and as soon as the big people ate then we could get some food for ourselves. I was one of the younger cousins and was affectionately called "Patty" instead of Pat. I hated that name, but everyone was bigger than me and I was simply an inconvenience.

I did, however, figure out how to get people to like me. Through my codependency, which extended not only to home but wherever I went, I learned that if I did the dishes, cleaned up the rooms we were in, offered to bring food or drinks to people they started to see me as someone they wanted around. I knew that I was conditionally loved but I knew that if they needed me, well, they would take care of me. I volunteered at church and would help anywhere and everywhere.

The third and final lesson we learn as kids is the lesson of self-efficacy. The belief that no matter what happened we could overcome it. This was a hard lesson for me to learn because my father was constantly belittling me. His favorite sayings were, "You could not drive a nail into soft wood" and "You could not hit the side of a barn if you were standing in front of it with a shotgun."

He kept pressing the fact that I could do nothing right, and it was a battle to even have a tiny bit of hope for the future.

I struggled with guilt, shame, fear, anger and pretty much every emotion that you could imagine. My identity was forming, and it was not looking too promising. The good and evil battle for my soul continued and a youth leader stepped up to the plate and started to really encourage me. He even got a lady at the church to buy me a new backpack and was going to take me, along with several other boys, on a campout to an island off the upper peninsula of Michigan. For a brief moment I felt special. I can remember the pride of packing that backpack for that trip and imagining that it might possibly be a good experience. By then I had this phobia about tents because usually when I was camping in one someone would crawl in and make me do sexual things to them or they would want to do sexual things to me.

After my father had been arrested, we had to spend a lot of time at my other Aunt's house as she would babysit my brothers and me. I hated going over there because they had lots of money, and it was always an adventure in futility. If I took a shower I got yelled at because I did not know how to dry myself off. If my aunt saw my underwear, they were never clean enough and she would pick them up and show everyone or pull them down so people could see for themselves.

My father and my aunt would stick a broomstick up our behind and laugh about it.

Demoralized, defeated, dejected. Somewhere in there was a message about God but Satan was doing his best to hide it behind the fog. Every time anything good happened, it was not too much longer when a tragedy would wipe it away.

Chapter Six

I tried my best to get through each day. For a while we lived in this one house that had a basement. I would crawl underneath the steps and set up my play area there. I did not want anyone to know because it was the only safe place for me. I would have some clay and pretend I was a dentist and would spend hours with my imagination.

As I got older there just was no escape from the sexual abuse, trafficking, and molestation. I was forced to do things to other boys and men, and they would have me stand at attention or wrap me up so that I could not move and do things to me.

I would want to vomit but there was no way out. This was my fate, and my only escape was to let my mind go elsewhere and do what they wanted because that way it would be over sooner. Even if I told my body to not react, there is a mechanism in boys that can cause arousal even if you do not want to be aroused. It only added to the confusion when something happened that you did not want but that something brought pleasure from the chemicals being released into the brain. It cemented the fact that it was what "I" wanted.

In sixth grade the church pastor told us all that we should get baptized and so because I was a people pleaser, I took the required classes that were taught by the pastor and then my relatives were all informed that I was going to be baptized. As a matter of fact, all the boys in my grade were going to be baptized but, on the day, when it was supposed to happen and we were showing up early at the church, no one else came. My schoolmates all backed out and I was too terrified to do anything but obey.

I got baptized, or at least I should say that I got dunked in a tank of water. Why they wanted to push me under water was oblivious to me, but I simply did what I was told.

But then I got to be a junior deacon at church. I had to dress up and then I got to help collect the offering plate. I was good at serving so there was a little bit of sunshine.

But back to the youth leader. I was in the youth group called "Pathfinders" and my new blue backpack was all packed up but then I started noticing that my mom was more tense than usual. I had just started 7th grade and the abuse had become just part of the ritual. "Get molested and then move on with life." "Grit my teeth and then start breathing again."

Yes, the nervous tics got worse but maybe the camping trip would help?

During this time, my father had been transferred to a minimum-security prison and we started having visits with him in a more park-like atmosphere. For years we went to visit my dad almost weekly at the large Jackson State Pen and even at the minimum security and the sounds of metal bars clanging together and the humiliation of being searched by the prison guards were now just a normal rhythm of life.

It does not take one long to be conditioned to the victim role. I knew as a small child that I had already been "marked" as a troublemaker just because of my dad. People joked about the name, "Nave." We were seen as those "no good" kids and the sense of crap invaded all of our souls. I had been teased, bullied, beaten, and abused and when I tossed in the way the law treated me in the prison, I knew that I was a worthless sh_t who had no hope for a good future. I can still feel the incredible sense of deep loss of identity and value.

When my dad was sent away my mother also gave birth to her youngest child, nine years my junior, and so we would haul Jason around wherever we went.

When my dad was transferred to the low-level security prison something changed inside of him, and a plan was hatched. In the Fall of 1977, right after school began and I entered the 7th grade and was selected to serve as a junior deacon at my church, my father escaped from prison.

My brothers and I did not know it at the time, but our lives would be forever scarred in a way that even we could ever imagine. I mean up until that point I did not think anything worse could happen in our lives. We had no stability, nothing good in our life, we were seen as crappy kids, and our friends were eventually told to leave us alone. We seemed to have some sort of evil letter carved on our foreheads and we were as low as one could get or so I thought.

In looking back at my life, it seemed like tragic, sad Lifetime or Hallmark channel movie. Bad thing after bad thing just kept happening and every time a small sliver of hope had begun to be seen, it was always dashed in some dramatic and powerful way. It was as if Satan was trying to tell me that I could never escape, that there was never going to be anything good for me. My life was doomed to be one of tragic pain and suffering and I could only imagine what the end would look like.

Yet I kept getting surprised as well. Just when you think it could not get any worse...it did.

My father's escape from prison was pretty simple in hindsight.

We packed up our station wagon and mom said we were going camping. I thought this was weird as I was getting ready to go camping with some people from church and had just packed my new backpack, which now my mom was telling me I could not take with me. She was acting really strange, and several relatives had come up to visit us but that was nothing new.

There was a weird tension in the home and when the relatives came to visit, they often exchanged words with my mother, and I did not know what was going on, but I knew that my mom really did not like the kinfolk much. After the relatives left, we continued on with our camping plans.

We all got in our station wagon and drove to where dad was living and I thought it was strange for us to camp in that neck of the woods but then my mom said to us, "look for your dad?" I had no idea as to what she meant as my dad was in prison, living in some cabin behind a tall fence. But my mom was resolute in her instructions, so we started looking out the window for my dad. We drove by once and didn't see anything and I really felt as though my mom was losing it but then she turned around and we drove back towards the prison and right before my eyes I saw my father and another guy, who we later learned was named Burt, running down a hillside carrying two large duffel bags.

Mom stopped the car, they pushed themselves into our car and we all managed to squeeze together like sardines and then we were off. No one said a word, and I was not breathing at the time. The car went quiet, and we just drove and drove. Eventually it started to get dark and still my mom did not stop driving the car. I had no idea which direction we were headed but eventually we spotted a sign that said, "Welcome to Indiana."

During the great escape we stopped to eat at a restaurant that was remarkably similar to a Denny's. We all packed into a booth and started nervously eating when a large group of police officers came into the restaurant to eat as well. The tension at our table shot up about 1000 degrees and I kept telling myself to keep looking at my food, I had reminded myself to swallow, and I was afraid we were about to have a shootout. I kept my eyes down and stared at my food. I did not want to eat but also did not want to attract attention.

I mean how do you act normal when your world is about to explode? In thinking back upon that day, I wonder if sweat was pouring down my face and my tics must have been going ballistic. We ate and quietly slipped out of the restaurant in one piece and then we drove further into Indiana and found ourselves driving around a large cemetery.

It was dark, foggy, and all around us were headstones and graves. My nerves were shot, I was in the midst of Red/Black trauma, and I just knew we were going to die in the cemetery. I was not sure if it was by the police or some zombie, but it was unnatural for us to be in such a place. We stayed there for a long time until some clock in my dad's head clicked, and it was time to go. Later I learned we had been at a monastery but all I remembered were gargoyles and vampires.

After hiding out among the gravestones we got back on the road and drove a little bit further. We drove into this old one-story motel and in the middle of the night scampered from our car to the small hotel room. When we got inside, we were introduced to Burt's family, who had driven to meet us there and there was another man who looked strangely similar to my dad. That man's last name was Kulwicki, and he ended up giving his driver's license over to my dad and from that moment on my dad told us that our last name was to now be Kulwicki.

I remember practicing the spelling of our new last name because I was afraid, once again, that if we got stopped and I was asked to spell it I would crack under the pressure and be responsible for sending my dad back to prison. I tried to make up a song for it, but my nerves were getting worse. K-U-L-W-I-C-K-I repeatedly.

The next three months found us staying in a tent in Greeley, Colorado and sleeping in our car at other times. We had no homes, no identity and were constantly being told not to make any friends and not to "talk to anyone." I want to say the time was exciting, but it was not. Terrifying was a more pervasive word as you have to imagine what living every day with the fear of being discovered felt like. We were all paranoid and I knew that I had to be careful because what if someone asked me my name and it slipped out that I was a "Nave." What if I froze when confronted by a police officer? Would I be shot? Was I now a criminal? Even though I had not done anything wrong it felt like I was the one being hunted.

Law enforcement was the enemy. We learned that after my dad had escaped the FBI was sent out to try to catch him. I am not sure how he knew but he kept bragging about all the times they tried to get us but missed.

We slowly worked our way across the United States until we reached Nevada. When we arrived in Vegas, we rented a tiny apartment in North Las Vegas with the other family that had escaped, and we attempted to survive. The tension was thick as we were packed into a two-bedroom mini apartment. There was a lot of secrecy, we could not go outside much and had to remain in hiding. The curtains were always shut, and we were told not to talk to anyone, not to make friends and so our little duplex apartment became our prison.

We were locked away in this prison apartment cell for a month or so and then my dad and Burt managed to find us a 27-foot travel trailer that had rolled over and was in need of repair. They purchased it and began to slowly fix it up. When it was completed, minus the bathroom, my dad moved us into a trailer park in North Las Vegas that was part of the Silver Nugget Casino and then he informed us that once again our name was going to change. This time we went from Kulwicki to Dumke and right away I hated it. Dumke was too close to donkey which I later found out was too close to jack ass and so the teasing began, this time for having a name that was not even mine.

The name Dumke had been chosen because my dad was going through a cemetery and found an infant that had died but was similar in age to him. He took that infant's name, William Dumke, and then we all got tagged as well.

We enrolled into a large inner city Vegas school and the very first day at the school I was beaten up by a guy for simply being a white kid in a mostly black school. It was agonizing and each day at school I was beaten up simply because of the color of my skin. I thought I was going to be killed. I was teased, threatened, and my books were constantly being stolen. Eventually one black kid stood up for me and I was able to relax a bit as long as I was around him.

We stayed in Vegas a few more months and then my dad and Burt decided that they needed to separate from each other, I guess to improve the odds of staying on the lamb. They chose California and my dad chose to head the other way. He had become friends with a deviant, pedophile guy from the trailer park who my dad bartered with. He could do whatever he wanted to my dad's kids and then the deviant guy would help my dad get what he needed to move out of state. This guy went out of his way to abuse kids and if it were today, I am sure he would have been wearing a clown suit and driving an ice cream truck.

While we were in Vegas my oldest brother got a job at McDonalds and we would anxiously await his arrival back home from work because he would bring with him the food that was thrown out by McDonalds, and we would eat it. Other times we would go to the garbage bins as well and grab some food. Our food system worked ok until the one night that food was brought home, and we ate it and then…my stomach started to churn, and I could not stop throwing up. We had been poisoned by old food and once again it just seemed like God had it out for me.

To this day I cannot eat any food that is close to the expiration date.

Chapter Seven

When January 1978 rolled around my parents packed up our travel trailer and with the help of the deviant we met in Vegas, we proceeded to drive from Las Vegas to Miami, Florida. The trip took about a month and was an experience in supernatural preservation.

We had barely gotten out of the Las Vegas area and found this little city called Needles and the deviant drove his RV into the soft sand and broke an axle. We all had to pull over on an Indian Reservation where eventually the people of the town warned us that if it rained, we would be washed away, great! We had to stay in that little area for a few days so that parts could be ordered and so we explored.

We panned for gold, found some, which my father promptly took from us. We ran around in the desert and just tried to stay away from the crazy guy and the trailer. We wanted to just be left alone.

Eventually the RV was fixed, and we were back on the road. We traveled the barren route 66 and went from one gas station to another. My one moment of joy was when we were able to get this used Star Wars book. The movie had recently come out and because we had no money there was no way we could watch it but the book, I could read, and I could imagine. I read it over and over again and found that my mind liked that escape.

We drove through several States and then we started to see the mountains and hills pass away and the flat lands of the south emerged. When we left Texas, we were then stuck in swampland and as we drove through Louisiana, the crazy guy, who was driving in front of us, had his trailer come off the hitch. Time slowed down as we saw it sway back and forth. It looked like it was going to plow right into us but at the last second it swerved sharply and disappeared into the swamp.

But the episode that stands out the most was when we finally got to Tampa and had to cross the largest bridge I had ever seen, the Sunshine Skyway. There was a lot of traffic, and we were moving slowly. But then just as we were about ¾ of the way up, the trailer that belonged to the crazy dude stopped. His RV broke down and right there on the bridge, my dad had to get under that thing and fix it. I still have nightmares about that bridge, and it did not help that a few months later the center part of the bridge collapsed.

For those of us who have experienced complex trauma, fear is often the right hand of our daily experience.

We continued our trip South after we made it over the bridge and ended up making camp in Bonita Springs. We did not have any money, so we found a place alongside the Gulf that was this little pullover area. We pulled over and just lived in the trailer there. While we lived in the trailer, dad and the crazy dude got jobs painting signs along the highway. I do not recall how long we stayed there but it was a month or two. Just enough time to save up some money and then we finally left the crazy guy behind and kept on driving to Miami.

Miami had been selected as a location because it was so transient and thus the perfect place to hide. We managed to find this large trailer park and so we moved into an area of Miami called Sweetwater.

We were so poor that when we entered Florida my foot started outgrowing my tennis shoes, which were the cheap version of the blue and white Starsky and Hutch shoes from television. We could not afford new shoes, so I first took a knife and cut out a hole for my toe to stick out, then the side of the shoes went, and I had to cut some more. Eventually, it took tape and a lot of luck to keep my shoes on my feet at all.

We lived at 9801 W. Flagler Avenue. I went to the area a little while ago and now it is a large community park. Back then it was a large mobile home and rv park. I was enrolled in the W.R. Thomas Jr. High School, and my brothers went to their schools. We were going to stay a while in Miami, so my parents moved forward with trying to establish some sort of normalcy.

My father, who was now Bill Dumke, got a job at a Ford dealership where he was the body shop foreman and life seemed to be as normal as it could be under the circumstances. Our main way of surviving was to stay out of the trailer for as long as we could. In Florida, the weather was pretty good and so we just tried to stay out and enjoy the life of living free.

In reality, we were anything but free. We had extremely strict rules which my father enforced with an iron fist. We could not tell anyone we met anything about our past. We could not talk about our parents or where we were from. We could never contact anyone who was a relative. No one was allowed into our living space, and we were not allowed to go into anyone else's living space either. We were expected to be model citizens and not to attract any unnecessary attention. We also had to have our windows closed, blinds drawn AT ALL TIMES, and we were instructed never to answer the phone.

We had the façade of freedom, but it was more like our father was a mini-Hitler. I am not sure if he meant well or not. I used to defend his actions saying that he needed to do what he did to protect us but as I grew older, I realized that everything my father did during this time was selfish. Ripping us out of school, dragging us around the United States, teaching us to lie-to hide-to never tell anything to anyone and the consistent emphasis that the law, the police were evil.

I do not know how we did it, but we survived the first few months of our transition to Miami, and I managed to finish the 7th grade school year. Then summer came and our dad rewarded us by moving into a single wide mobile home in the same trailer park and it was like winning the lottery. Now we could move around and had a nice toilet, two toilets, a shower and a big fridge that worked. We had finally made it to the "big time." We parked our little travel trailer next to our trailer and it was a token of moving on up in the world.

About this same time my dad made friends with an insurance guy who was as crooked as he could be. His name was Vince and Vince exposed my dad to the organized crime scene in South Florida, which during the late 70's and early 80's was a drug dealers dream come true. In fact, a documentary has been made of that time entitled, "Cocaine Cowboys" and even that documentary did not do justice to the times of South Florida during this stretch of history. Vince was from Cuba and had ties to all sorts of shady characters who soon took a liking to my father.

It did not take long for my dad to quit his job at the Ford dealership and to start working for one of the shady dudes that he had met through Vince. He started out working at a furniture store that was run by the mob and Alfredo, and then he got promoted to some sort of chop shop auto body repair facility, where I also got to work and then he was promoted again, this time he was a body guard or better known as an enforcer for Alfredo. Wherever Alfredo went, my dad went. It was this last promotion that set up my father for a life of high criminal activity.

Alfredo was a cruel and ruthless drug dealer, and he had no patience for anyone who would get in his way. He was busy building an empire and during the great Miami riots in 1980, my dad was Alfredo's bodyguard as he ventured throughout the tragedy that came to be known as Little Havana. Thousands were hurt, hundreds killed as the national guard was called in to restore order. Alfredo thrived during this time and as he became more influential so did my father.

As my father progressed up the criminal steps and as I got to work alongside him at the crooked furniture store and auto body shop, it became all too clear what my father was capable of doing. He started carrying guns and knives, wearing cowboy boots, not sleeping well, using drugs, and drinking heavily. It seemed that quite regularly my father would overdose, and I would have to spend hours walking him around, putting ice on his wrists and forehead and doing everything I could to keep him alive.

His nickname became Peter Rabbit and to us my father became more of an evil fairy tale. He would come home with a briefcase full of money almost every night and I would be called upon to count it. I can recall counting millions of dollars nightly and wishing that some of it were mine but knowing that if I took a single dollar, it would potentially cost me my life.

Our lives grew out of control and in a few short years my dad had worked his way up to becoming a creative drug dealer. He worked alongside several different drug dealers who did not like each other but they all liked my dad. As a result, my dad started making greater and greater connections. He worked for Alfredo, Bud the hillbilly, and Little. I often traveled with my father, and he would always tell me that I was not to say anything about any of the other drug dealers to the other ones. I was to keep my mouth shut so I learned early on to zip my lip and observe.

When I was around Bud, I learned how to launder drug money through farming. Bud was this "good old boy" from the back woods, and he had a twang that was often difficult to decipher. He lived in this cool townhouse north of Miami and had a television that covered the wall. Bud owned pig farms scattered all the way from Hialeah to Okeechobee and he showed me how to launder money with legitimate businesses and they also said that if you wanted to get rid of someone there was nothing better than wild pigs.

The drug profits went through the farms and the pig stench was the perfect cover for what was transpiring. With Alfredo, I learned about running crooked businesses and laundering money through other avenues and the power of intimidation. Alfredo had many Cuban connections throughout South Florida, and he owned laundromats, auto repair stores, furniture stores and the like. I often hung out with one of Alfredo's guys, Rafael, whose sole job was to mix up creative explosive concoctions that would be used to intimidate those who chose to oppose Alfredo's growing empire.

Alfredo would throw parties and rent out entire floors of hotels on the beach. He would light bottle rockets and launch them inside and he was always drinking a Michelob, which seemed to be the beer of choice for drug dealers in South Miami.

Little was the strangest of the bunch. He was very guarded, and you did not see him out much. He ran things from his large house on the outskirts of Miami and when I was taken to his house my dad would position me in the horse barn near the feed. I had a Mac-10 machine gun available to me at that location and my father told me to scan the field behind the house and if I saw anyone moving out back to start firing as fast as I could.

I felt like Clint Eastwood in one of his spaghetti westerns and I also felt important. Within my grasp was great power as a gun meant that I could dictate the future around me. I learned what fear was all about and how to channel that fear into control and power. I also learned what living under the threat of constant death did to you. Many of my dad's friends were killed, murdered and as I hung around them more and more, I knew that at any time something bad could happen, so you always had to be prepared and ready.

I studied what made the men successful. I wanted to know how this one could seemingly dodge prison and that one would always end up in trouble?

I met a cast of characters. There was the Jeweler who did time for those above him and was rewarded with a jewelry store in Miami and a pension for life. He was always going around with a large joint in his mouth and as he passed by you, he would stick it in your mouth and say, "take a hit." He was around 5 foot tall and probably about 5 feet around as well. He would tell stories of being loyal, of the mob taking care of you, etc.

Whether it was driving like madmen through the mountains of North Carolina transporting illegal substances and hoping to not get caught or running drugs in Miami I had the opportunity to hang around murderers, thieves, drug dealers, and women that were beautiful and who were only after one thing—power. It was a surreal life and one that I would find myself enjoying more and more. It was a nervous and anxious way to live, a dangerous way to live as many who tried their hand in this field either got killed or arrested. Most had a short life span but the few that somehow were able to navigate it though lived lives of luxury. It was worse odds than playing the lotto, but I thought that I was clever enough to escape the law and as I hung around all these people a plan for my future was soon hatched. A plan that involved making enough money to have anything I ever wanted.

Chapter Eight

One of my friends was Freddy. Freddy's dad was the equivalent of my godfather, and he took me in under his wing. Freddy's dad, Bud, would give me a Bayer Aspirin container full of pure cocaine every time I saw him and so by the time I reached the age of 16, I was driving a stolen car, carrying a knife in my boot, talking with an attitude, using cocaine and drinking large quantities of Vodka just to start my day and life started losing interest. I also had lost all sense of fear and pretty much felt as though I was invincible.

There was an incident with a gun that illustrated just how "numb" I had gotten. It was late at night and in this little park there were about 10 people getting wasted. There was this young man, actually, probably a year older than me, who was higher than a kite. He had this revolver out swinging it around and it seemed as though he was determined to shoot someone to show his coolness and power. After watching him for a while it aggravated me and so I walked up to him, and he placed the gun to my chest. I felt no fear, I felt "nothing," and I simply ignored his threats and took the gun out of his hands.

The Bible in 2 Corinthians 4:4 talks about the god of this world blinding our eyes. At this point in my life my eyes were blinded and even though God kept trying to push in I did my best to keep Him out. Yet, when I look back, I can see how God protected me time after time.

Bud taught me the finer elements of life and introduced me to many influential people. One man in particular was 19 years old and was a hit man for the mob. That meant his job was to eliminate people that were deemed to be "in the way" of progress. He sought to eliminate them by taking their lives from them. I asked him about his trade, and he told me he only carried a single shot rifle. I told him that was pretty stupid because what if he missed but he told me that he never missed. I thought that was pretty cool and so I put up on my list of possibilities, "Hit man."

Bud told me that I could do whatever I wanted, and he would support me which was great except for one thing. Bud and my dad had a falling out over my father's developing greed and lust. Bud told me that my dad would chase any skirt who had a lot of money and that my dad was addicted to money and power. Bud offered to help me in spite of my dad, and I agreed.

I became Bud's traveling representative and football analyst. I would do errands for Bud and in return he would give me money. I never had to ask about the errands and whether it was picking up a package, working on his pig farm, or just sitting down and telling him who would win football games I would do what I was asked and took my place as the up-and-coming youngster. I won large sums of money for him for which he paid me off with a decent cash payout and then gave me a custom knife and a really nice Winchester 30/30 rifle (pre-1964). He loved me like a son, and I would later use that connection to my own advantage.

My father meanwhile was rapidly rising in the ranks of organized crime, getting in with the Cuban and Haitian refugees that were coming into Miami at the time and my dad joked about being part of the "cocaine cowboys." A term that was designated for those who defended the illegal drug trade with reckless abandon.

Miami was a hodge podge of drug and gang wars and when you turned on the news you could see people from Haiti arriving on the beach in boats and running for freedom. Little Havana was a section of Miami that was especially volatile. There were many who had escaped from the clutches of Fidel Castro and they did not want to be taken advantage of again. Castro had cleaned out his prisons and had sent many of the deranged people over to the United States via boats.

When they arrived in Miami these people were herded up and soon, they were placed in a large, fenced camp underneath the expressway that became their home away from home. We would drive over that section of the highway and see this huge tent city below us and one could only imagine the terrible things that were being done.

During this time, I went through Little Havana and my crazy father got drunk, went into the Cuban radio station, and held a gun up to the host of the radio station and even though he could not speak Spanish proclaimed a message of freedom for the masses. I did not expect my father to return from that trip, but he had no fear and somehow people respected him.

My father used to brag about the people he had killed, the women he had slept with, and the deals he had made. As a result of living in this sort of life my older brother became a nervous wreck and had to leave and went up to Michigan to live with Granny, which left me to hold everything together and I fell in love with making everything work, I was indeed the savior of my family and I sought to keep everyone safe and secure. I stepped into the dad role for my youngest brother, and I tried to balance life and my desire to make it on my own.

Drugs and alcohol were the main way we all stayed sane during this time. We had great access to both and there was not a day that went by that we were not aware that someone could be out tracking us. Whether it was the government hunting for my dad, the drug dealers trying to get revenge, or someone else trying to muscle their way up in the ranks of unorganized crime. We were taught to fear the police and be leery of anyone who seemed to only want to do good. They were both manipulators and hypocrites. The criminals, on the other hand, could sometimes be trusted. Yes, I know it was a twisted mind.

My dad and I were out working on a car one day when across the sky some ducks were flying and I yelled out to my dad, "Duck!" He hit the ground as he thought someone was shooting and that described the tension that we were all under. Another time we were driving a big old Lincoln down the interstate, and someone was chasing us, and we were dodging cars and trying to escape. The tension was palpable and always surrounded us.

There was never a moment when you could relax. There was always someone that wanted to work their way up the South Miami drug scene and you were always the person in the way. You could trust no one, you could not sleep without having one eye open and if you ever dared think that someone cared for you, well, it was the beginning of the end.

Dad would take many trips into the Everglades and was part of a crew that would walk through the glades picking up drugs that had been dropped out of the sky by pilots flying back from South America. I think this was when my fear of gators started to grow because when one was in the everglades you were aware that there were alligator nests under the water and we had been told that a gator would be able to grab you and drag you down into its underground bunker while you were still alive. I was never sure if this was true or not, but it planted seeds of fear regardless.

During my ninth-grade year, as I described earlier, I was working at a chop shop in downtown Miami and helping deliver furniture in Little Havana. I had managed to learn the majority of Spanish cuss words and was enjoying my time of hanging out with drug dealers and drinking the official soft drink of South Miami, Michelob beer.

Gangs had infiltrated the Junior High school I attended, and I was invited to be a part but from my perspective the school gangs were not as powerful as the adult version, so I turned down their invitation and hung out with my dad. I went to school, worked with my dad, and slowly got immersed more and more into the drug culture.

I also started hanging out with Freddy and we developed our own little ritual. It would start out drinking a couple of Stroh's beers, that would be followed by some German Beer, and then we would break out the cocaine and tequila. I can remember attempting to drive home from Hialeah to Miami after one such adventure and having the highway disappear and reappear. The powerful effects of cocaine and alcohol really warped one's sense of reality and many times I cheated death through some strange concoction.

While under the influence I did many stupid things. I would drive like a maniac, spin the car in circles at the intersection, challenge anyone around me, walk up to people holding guns and take hold of them. I even got into a few fights where I would black out with rage and then suddenly "snap out of it."

As my dad's tenure and position in the South Miami crime scene increased so did mine. I was making connections with the movers and shakers, meeting judges and politicians. In South Miami in the late 70's and early 80's there were many political individuals who were always serving the people through the lens of whoever gave them the most money. Reputations were built by keeping this person out of jail for so much money and you could tell that money and drugs ruled South Florida.

In my mind I was planning my entrepreneurial rise to the top. I would hang out at Bud's townhouse, which was pretty much a party that never ended, and soak up whatever information that I could gather. I would see how quickly alliances would be built and then later destroyed. There were drugs, alcohol, and women of various types everywhere. People would come in, flop down for a bit, and then head back out.

When you sat down you had to make sure that you were not sitting on someone's gun or flirting with someone's girlfriend for the day or night, whichever the case may be. I drove around from gravel pits to pig farms, to stores that served as fronts for some criminal element or out to some mansion to meet with strange people with even stranger methods of conducting business.

There was always someone who had just gotten shot or who had been killed and the corruption of the times ran rampant. I think if you were to look up the statistics for Dade County during this time you would see the excess of crime. Dade County became the joke of the nation and even made the cover of Time Magazine.

During the hay day of the drug wars, a group of FBI agents were gunned down outside of a bank and the drug dealers had no fear of any authority. My dad and I watched the television news coverage of the massacre and laughed while we told ourselves, "They deserved it."

There were more crooked cops than straight ones, politicians were corrupt, senators had been bought, and if you were not involved in something illegal it seemed as if you were the strange one.

Now one of the side benefits of having a drug dealer for a father was that word soon drifted out in the neighborhood and no one messed with you. Everyone feared my father. One time our neighbor was outside and was yelling at my brother who was in the little neighborhood park. My mom went out to calm the situation down and the man turned on my mother and started screaming at her. It was more than my dad could take and so he burst out of the door and stalked up to the man and stood up on his tippy toes and got in the guy's face.

The man would not back down and said to my father, "What are you doing to do, kill me?" My dad, with anger tattooed on his face simply replied with clenched teeth, "that can be arranged, sport." The man panicked and ran back into his house, and I just stuck my chest out letting everyone know that clearly, "my dad could take their dad any day!"

Chapter Nine

Near the end of my tenth-grade year my father was finally tracked down by the FBI and was arrested by Agent Donahue. The arrest involved a silent campaign whereby the feds evacuated a large part of the trailer park and had the manager of the park, Mim, call my mother on the phone so that she would come up to the office. My two brothers and I were all at school, so the feds knew that my dad was alone in the trailer.

My mom told me that as she walked to the office, which was not that far from where we lived, she started to feel uneasy, noticed that no one was around and when it dawned upon her what was happening tried to dash back to warn my dad, but it was too late. The feds grabbed her and made their approach.

When they surrounded the trailer, they informed my dad that he was surrounded and gave him a choice to come out, unarmed, with his hands in the air. I know my dad entertained the thought of going out firing like Butch Cassidy and the Sundance Kid but they had caught him in one of his hung over and sane, melancholy moments so he actually did what they asked. Before he went out, he hid some money and guns under the bed but then he just got up and walked out.

The cops converged and after years of living on the run he was now officially "captured."

The drama moved quickly and as soon as my dad was removed from the premises, the quarantine was lifted, and people came back into the area. A few hours later when I had finally gotten home from Track-n-Field practice at the high school I noticed that things seemed a little too quiet. I usually did not have any sense of anything like that, but something just did not seem right. I carefully parked my bike and went inside the trailer and as I did, I looked around and no one was home. That did not surprise me too much as I always got home earlier than my brothers but where was my mom? I went into the kitchen and that is when I knew the crap had hit the fan. I knew this because on the kitchen table was a business card from an FBI agent named Donahue.

I knew that there would be no way we would have a card like that in our house, so I quickly surmised that either my dad had been caught or he was on the run again. I did not know if that meant we were now on our own in Miami?

I did not know if my mom and Dad had taken off leaving me in charge? There were no cell phones, and I had not talked to a relative in a long time and there was no way I was going to place a call to the police to ask what had happened, so I was left with that choice that no one likes, waiting.

Eventually mom returned and told me what had happened. Dad had been arrested and transported off to the City of Miami jail. He had been arrested for fleeing the State of Michigan and escaping from prison but strangely enough was never charged with anything else because the Fed's just thought he had become a good, all American pig farmer. Go figure!

Over the next few months my father went through several court appearances dressed in a bright orange jump suit and we managed to visit him weekly in the Dade County Jail, which brought us all back to those Jackson Prison days. This time when we would visit him, we were searched and had to be escorted through the metal bars but had to sit in a small space where we could talk to dad through a heavy mesh grate at the bottom of a window.

It was not the best, but it was all that was allowed.

Dad had informed me through his phone calls and in our visits that some people might be coming to the house to ask some questions. I was told to be on the alert and sure enough, it was only a few days later when a plain brown car pulled up and a couple of guys got out right when I got home from school.

They were both wearing suits and looked like they were police officers, but you could tell from the look in their eyes that if they were cops, they probably were a little bit on the crooked side. I tried to ignore them, but they followed me into our fenced in yard and then shut the gate behind them. They turned to face me and positioned themselves between me and the door to our trailer, and one pulled back his jacket to show me he was carrying a gun.

I had a weird feeling and as they started grilling me about the whereabouts of Bill Dumke, who they did not know was also Jim Nave. I was terrified but all those years of lying to survive came in handy and so I lied to them as well. They asked me where my father was, I told them he was out. They asked me when I would see him next. I told them I never knew when he would pop in. They asked me what type of car he was driving, and I made one up on the spot. No matter what the question, my panicked brain came up with a convincing answer and then they decided to do something but before they could reach me the older lady who lived behind us appeared like a guardian angel.

She had no idea what was going on but she was a feisty woman and so she started screaming that she was going to call the cops. She was like a mad hen and was yelling, screaming and the guys started to approach her but then suddenly, they turned, looked at me once more and said to tell my dad they would be back and then they left in this non-descript brown car.

They cussed her out and threatened her as well and after they were gone and my legs stopped shaking, I let go of my bike, thanked the lady who wanted to know what was going on, but I really did not know. She told me that if I needed anything to let her know and then I climbed up the steps and unlocked the door to our trailer where I was shocked by what was inside. My mom and brothers were in the trailer and all hunkered down, hiding. My mom had left me to hang, and I just could not believe it.

I guess I could not blame her. Life with my dad was anything but calm. My mom had been involved in fist fights, threats and who knows what else, so I figured if she was hiding there had to be a good reason.

Life continued onward with my dad in jail and me thinking that each time I went home someone was going to jump me. I started taking different routes and being careful to make sure that I was not being followed. I figured that dad owed some guys some money or something and I knew that he had come up with at least $20,000 from someone and hidden it under the bed. Secretly, I had wished that my dad had stashed the million-dollar briefcase under the bed but that never happened.

As the court procedure started dragging onward and people started to understand that my dad was nowhere to be seen, the other drug dealers in the area started circling. There was no honor among thieves, and they sensed that something was amiss.

It culminated one night when my dad called and told me someone was coming to visit. I knew what that meant. Before my father had been caught, he had instructed me what to do if he ever told me that someone was coming. It involved locking down inside the house, moving all the cars to the far side of the street and flipping the couch over and slouching down behind it with my eyes on the doorknob. If the doorknob turned, I was to fire. My dad had placed several guns throughout the house, but he had this sweet little sawed-off shotgun which was supposed to be my weapon of choice.

I did as he had instructed and waited. My mom and grandmother were there, and they sensed that something was really wrong, so they backed off and all night long I waited for the knob to turn. My blood pressure was pumping, and I kept repeating to myself what I was to do after I shot whoever was coming through the door.

I was to grab the briefcase of money, grab the guns and go out the back door and run. I was to go to the canal by an elementary school, wipe down the guns, take out the bullets and then call a lady whose number had been given to me and I had to memorize. She was to fly me out and so a plan was in motion and all I could do was wait. It involved protecting my family so that was all that mattered.

The night continued and soon day broke and there was no incident. I never did find out what happened, but the threats declined after that night.

Months dragged on and eventually my dad was ordered to be extradited back to Michigan. The summer had passed, and we learned that dad was going back to Jackson State Prison. I could not believe it. The place he had escaped was now his new destination and so they took him off, shackled head to toe, in some small plane that hit about every storm you could hit before crashing. My dad later told me that he was sure they were all going to die from the storm.

While he was gone my two younger brothers and mother coped the best we could. We had no income, but my dad did have a briefcase under the bed with cash in it and my mom started working in her now, legal name. It was a very tense time, and no one seemed to know what to do. My mom divorced my dad, and we were left to try to figure out what it all meant.

Eventually, I decided that I wanted to be closer to my dad and so I moved to Michigan and ended up living with my Granny. I got a job at a local pizza restaurant and proceeded to enroll into the 11th grade at Pontiac Northern Senior High School.

It was a tough transition going from the world of crime to one where my Granny tried to bring us up right. I now had rules, no money, was stuck in a climate that got cold and when I worked cleaning off tables at the pizza place, I kept thinking how much I could be making if I were back in Miami. I mean what a waste of time. I could not see how anyone could want to be legit because there did not seem to be much money in it.

My relatives tried to help and offered reassuring words, but no one ever suggested talking to a counselor and I do not know if I would have if someone did suggest it. From my perspective life was a big pile of crap.

While I was at Northern High School four kids came up behind me and broke my jaw in several places. I was hit with brass knucks, and I was out of school for a month while I healed. Since it was my jaw that was broken it could not be put into a cast, but they could wire my mouth shut so that it would heal in place. After they did the procedure, the doctor told me to always carry a pair of wire cutters because if I got sick and threw up, I would drown, which was such a pleasant thought.

I managed to finish off my classes with the schools help but the hatred in me went bezerk. It was like I told you, just when you thought it could not get any worse it did. Now it was my health that was being impacted and I was "pissed."

As soon as my jaw was wired shut my cousin and I went out looking for the guys who broke my jaw. We had taken a rifle and a pistol along with us and if we could have found them, I would have killed them. There was only hatred in my heart, and I wanted revenge.

We spent the day hunting but unfortunately, we did not find them. I had to settle with thoughts of doing them harm, but it was not enough. I lost the spark in my eyes and there became a dull evil that just would not go away. What I did not fully understand at the time was the life of hatred and crime that had permeated my family history.

Chapter Ten

Even though I had witnessed the powerful negative effects of a life of crime in my own immediate family and knew the heritage of my family it was not until I was an adult that I did some genealogical research and discovered, much to my chagrin, the full picture.

We were directly related to Jesse James who roamed the hills of Missouri around the time of the Civil War. As a matter of fact, Jesse's dad was a preacher who tried to keep his son on the neat and narrow, but Jesse had a wild hair and decided to ride with those who stood against President Lincoln and the Northerners.

In the history of the State of Missouri, during the time when the State had to declare allegiance to either the north or the south, Missouri was leaning South. President Lincoln did not want to lose the State, so he convinced the immigrants in St. Louis to vote and support the North and they did. The result was that the contingent from St. Louis voted for the North and the rest of the State went South. A civil war was launched in the State and President Lincoln gave the orders that whatever had to be done to convince the rest of the State to side with the North would be allowed.

History tells us of the times that the Northern troops would gather up women and children and burn them alive to convince their husbands and fathers to help the North. However, instead of turning the hearts towards the North the men became all the more determined to overthrow it and Jesse James rode with one such man, William Contrell.

It was a bloody time and one of the blood thirstiest men of that era was a man named Jim Nave, the same name as my father. Jim was a man who had murdered and pillaged and sought revenge against the north. Eventually he was caught and sentenced to die but he escaped and then eventually was caught and killed. The similarity between him and my dad was creepy.

The distrust for the government ran deep in our bones and that heritage of crime and mistrust only grew through the years

Unfortunately, it was not only in the Missouri area that we found our great lineage to a life of crime. We were also related to one of the members of the ruthless Purple Gang in Detroit, the only gang that Al Capone feared, and had members of the family in organized crime through the mafia in Detroit as well. My dad used to drive me by the place that Jimmy Hoffa had disappeared, and I was taught that the Unions were as ruthless as could be.

I had many relatives that worked on the wrong side of the police force and the stories that I soaked up had me thinking that I was born to be an outlaw. I knew that the majority of the men in our family had done time in jail or prison, but I really felt as though I was smarter than the average "joe." I would spend my time thinking, pondering, analyzing, and figuring out ways in which to make the organized crime life pay and eliminate the risk of being caught. My favorite scenario involved robbing a bank and I had pretty much figured it out but never got the chance to attempt it, which in hindsight I realize was only due to the grace of God.

By the time Christmas break rolled around, some three months after I had gone up to Michigan to be closer to my dad, I had had enough of the straight life and so I determined to make my mark. I got in touch with Bud back in Miami and started helping him again bet on various sporting events. I also contacted Vince, my dad's friend, and set up a cocaine buy and sell, and even managed to purchase a large truck load of marijuana coming from the west coast. I was busy wheeling and dealing, then bought airline tickets and flew from Detroit to Miami without my grandmother knowing. I was tired of the "good life" and wanted to get back in the game.

When I arrived in Miami I was greeted by a friend, Carlos, who was driving a new Cadillac, and I wasted no time setting the plan into full motion and enjoying the finer things of Miami as well. I drove his caddy, ate the finest food, and purchased the best coke I could find. I rented a couple of rooms at a hotel and pretty much partied as often as I could.

On the trip back to Miami, I brought with me my dad's hot box, which was a small wooden electronic device that resembled a case that held a fifth of whiskey. When you opened it up there was an LED display and a place to put a sample of cocaine where it would be heated up and measured for purity. Just having one guaranteed some time in jail, but it was a necessary part of a big-time drug deal. You did not want to purchase any cut drugs because that would reduce your profit.

I had a thousand cash in my pocket to keep me afloat, my hot box, and so I stopped off at a Cuban meat market and made my initial purchase of coke and went back to my hotel room to test it out. If it measured high, I would make a larger purchase and then proceed to mix it and resell it to my friend Carlos, who was running a distribution center and many ways to get the drug out to the people of South Miami.

The marijuana was on its way, and I could see the money that was about to be made. I ordered a large amount of food and set about planning a large party and it was while the party was going full bore that I noticed Vince, my dad's friend, slip off. He eventually ended up flying up to Michigan to see my dad in prison, or so he said, and it slowly dawned upon me that Vince was up to no good and was set to throw my plans off. I never was sure if my dad had told him to mess with me or he did it on his own but within a week I was out hunting him and if I had found Vince, I do believe he would have been dead.

My big drug deal fell apart, and it was probably a good thing as I learned later that the Feds had been watching me, but I was a bit naïve at the time and sure that I could have pulled it all off. After the aborted drug deal, I ended up staying in front of the Publix supermarket for two days without eating or drinking anything. I had a suitcase under my feet, knives in my boots and a hotbox in the suitcase and I just did not know what to do.

The next day one of my dad's ex-girlfriends had a guy show up to come get me and he took me back to where my mom was living and dropped me off. My mom had no clue that I was even in Miami as she had divorced my dad and was living as far from him as she could in a different mobile home but in the same neighborhood where we had all lived previously.

I ended up staying with my mom at her trailer for a while and life became all about how much vodka I could consume to start my day. I would start my day with a big gulp full of vodka and sip away until the morning passed, and all pain and agony of spirit was drowned. Life no longer made any sense to me and as I reflected upon my short life it had already measured up to tragic levels. No matter how hard I looked I just could not see any hope, no way out.

The only direction I could even begin to see was the path of self-destruction. I would drink, use any drugs I could find, do stupid things to assure myself that I was still alive and pretty much go around with a death wish.

There were times when I would walk up to a drunken guy brandishing a gun and would tell him to either shoot me or give me the gun. I talked people out of doing many things and went through life in a depressed haze.

My self-destructive path was rapidly gaining speed and as I limped through the summer it was becoming apparent that if I did not make a change for the better, I would probably end up dead. I had reached the point where I just did not care about anything.

I did not smile, felt no joy, and knew that society saw me as a piece of garbage. I had no idea what to do but deep within my soul was this truth that my grandmother had planted there. When we were little, she would read us the Bible Stories out of the Bible. Every night she would tell us about them, and we were forced to listen. Even though I did not want to hear them they stuck deep inside and so even though I did not want anything to do with God, I did know that Satan was real.

As a result, I would try to make deals with the devil and would tell him that if he would just take away the pain, I would do anything for him. I needed money and fame, wealth, and power, but fortunately, God blocked that request and even though I ended up far from Him, He never ended up far from me.

Chapter Eleven

I survived living with my mom for several months before my younger brother and I decided to go back to Michigan to be with my Granny and to be closer to my dad. We were told that we were going to be enrolled in a private, high school, Christian boarding Academy in Holly, Michigan, because my family was worried about whether my Granny could take care of us all. We flew to Detroit and hung out at Granny's house until school started and then we were driven up to Holly where we were enrolled in the Adelphian Academy boarding school and informed of all the rules.

We enrolled but it was hard. I was used to living fairly freely but the school had a rule for everything. You had to be in your room by this time, the lights had to be turned off at that time. You could only walk on the sidewalk for boys, could not hold the hand of any girl or you would be punished, and no music was allowed because they thought we might be tempted to listen to that Satanic rock music. I was at a low point during this transition so I was open to the idea that things might turn around for me. I thought I would try this religion thing, at least for a few weeks.

We were required to attend church and chapel meetings daily. We had to dress up in clothes that were "not jeans" in nature. Most of the kids at the school came from money so there was this incredible peer pressure to be snotty and fashionable. The school operated under this façade, and you could tell that most people were being fake, but no one would admit to it. My roommate, Rick, and I were about as far from God as one could be so we would sit on the front row and tease the speaker. One time the speaker grew so frustrated that after his talk he asked to speak to my friend and I and chewed us out for disrespecting him. Ha, he was in for a surprise because it was not just him that we disrespected but it was everyone.

My cousin would smuggle in big macs from McDonald's, which was contraband on that vegetarian campus, and on most weekends, I could be found drinking orange vodka on the steps to the gymnasium while unsuspecting faculty walked all around. I tried my best to fit in, but I saw too much hypocrisy from my own point of view and decided that I had to get out of there. As an interesting side note, everyone at the school was so busy seeing people and students as they appeared that no one thought about getting below the surface.

The school was aware of who my father was and had heard some of my life story and yet they never once asked, "How I was doing." They just kept doing their routine and I went around as invisible on that campus. They were quick to pass blame and judgment, but their approach only served to push behaviors deeper down.

The epitome of my time at the boarding school, which incidentally was a mere two months, happened strangely enough on the football field. I was a senior at that time and the boys were told to select a flag football team which would then play the faculty in an all-star game. I was a very good athlete so was chosen as the captain, so I got to pick the team and we went out intent on destroying the faculty. We were winning the game until one of my friends started running down the sideline with the ball and the religion teacher, who also just happened to be the chaplain of the school illegally clothes lined my friend, Michael.

My friend went down and bounced up like a rocket and was about to tear the faculty member's head off, but I intervened only to have it happen to me a few plays later. I looked at that chaplain guy and thought if that is how a Christian is supposed to behave, then it is all bull.

After two months of trying to fit in, my roommate and I, both at the wise old age of 17, packed up our duffle bags, climbed the back fence of the school, and walked off the school grounds and hiked into the downtown area of Holly, Michigan. Once we were there, we found these two girls at a pizza restaurant who gave us a ride to Pontiac, which was about 45 minutes away, and from there we hitch hiked to Canada and ended up almost getting arrested by Mounties for wading into the edge of the Niagara Falls, not the brightest thing to do. By now you should be getting a feeling it happened a lot.

It was while we were in Canada that Rick and I were forced to do sexual things or face an uncertain future and the trauma of being trafficked for sex still haunts me to this day. One can say they would never do this or that but when faced with survival a person can be forced to do the unthinkable. It was do this or be arrested. Do this or go to jail in Canada. I did what I needed to do to survive.

Rick and I survived for a couple of weeks on a loaf of bread and a package of bologna and drank as much coffee as we could because we got free refills, and we could add as much sugar as we could for nutrition. We also bummed cigarettes and did our best to smoke to keep warm. We made the trip from Canada to Miami in the back of a pickup truck and rain or shine we were back there trying to survive and keep from being blown out, which proved to be quite the experience when driving through the wavy mountain roads of West Virginia or the downpours of the Carolina's.

We arrived in Miami without any of my relatives knowing where I was at and slept in some trees on a golf course and tried to adjust to our new homeless state. We eventually ended up living at my mom's trailer with my youngest brother, Jason. Rick and I both got jobs at a landscaping company, and we did what we could to once again "survive." Rick managed to hang out in Florida for a month and then he took a bus back to Michigan and that was the last I ever heard from him.

I tried my best to adjust to life back in Miami, but it was difficult, and I quickly got back on a track towards self-destruction. I got into my pitiful pattern of getting drunk in the morning and sleeping all time away. I would get up and lift some weights and drink some more. Life seemed rather hopeless and in the midst of my despair my father called one day from prison with a business opportunity.

He had a grand plan which involved kidnapping my baby brother and taking him into hiding. Since I didn't have anything else going on at the time I agreed, so this lady, Joette, showed up in a really nice white Mercedes and off to the airport we went.

We flew off to North Carolina where we lived a life of luxury for about three weeks. We stayed at Paul's house, which was this beautiful mansion outside of Cherokee. The house had a glass front that peered out over the valley and there were several guests there who were staying for a wild New Year's Eve party. I have to admit that this was the first and last time that I got sick from drinking too much or drinking something that I had no idea what it was. It was not a wonderful experience sitting in a public restroom, leaning on the sink trying to throw up and being so sick even that would not work.

While I was in North Carolina a jeweler, Big Mike, came up from Florida to help out and all he seemed to do was walk around the estate with a huge

"Cheech and Chong" marijuana joint in his mouth. It was the largest "joint" I had ever seen and every time he passed by; he would offer me a hit. Paul's wife kept telling me stories of Elvis, as she had grown up with the "King" and I found myself thinking that I wanted to just stay here and hang out forever.

I had my run of the place and quickly fit in. Paul arranged for me to have spending money and so I would buy stuff, party, hang out, go for walks in the hills, and breathe in the crisp air. Jason, my little brother, was having fun as well. He had been living in a stuffed up little trailer in Miami and now he had hills to run and places to explore. We could have lived there forever but as they say, "all good things come to an end."

Our time was cut because my dad had been thrown into solitary confinement in prison because it had been alleged that he had something to do with the kidnapping of Jason, my youngest brother. As a result, my dad told me to fly back to Miami and drop off Jason and then fly to Michigan where I was to hide out while the police continued looking for me. I really did not have any choice and it turned out to be one of the hardest things that I ever had to do, taking my little brother back to Miami and leaving him there alone. I felt like I was his dad and I wanted to protect him but couldn't.

When I got to Michigan, I went into hiding at my Aunt Wanda's house in Clarkston, Michigan fearing that I might be discovered and charged with being a kidnapper. I did not know what was going on, there was no internet to check, so all I could do was lay low. No one could know where I was at, and I could not talk to my little brother who I missed so much. It did not take very long for the charges to be dropped and life was then back to normal.

I ended up living at Granny's once again, this time with my two brothers who had gone off the religious deep end and were attending these Revelation Seminar meetings at the local Church and I just knew that they had gone crazy. I teased them relentlessly and tried to discourage them from being "religious." I went to church because that was the deal for staying at Granny's, but I tried my best to not learn anything.

A God who would let little boys be raped and beaten, a God who would let women get raped, a God who would allow federal agents to get murdered for simply trying to do their job? It seemed as though God was on vacation or just did not care. There is a belief called Deism which goes like this. God created the world and spun it into action and then he simply stood aside and let it all play out. That was my view of God. He may have created the world, but he sure was doing a terrible job of running it.

My favorite position at church was outside of the morning worship service near the bathroom. Somehow, I felt the need to roam the hallway, step outside for a moment, anything but sit in the pews at church. I mean, really, who does that?

Meanwhile, the inner rage that I felt was brewing and growing which I know is hard to imagine. You would think that at some point it would top off, but my reservoir of rage and anger potential was apparently quite large. It was like a cancer inside of me that created a foggy filter from which I viewed the world. I was angry at the hand that life had dealt me, and I did not trust people one iota.

I ended up graduating from Pontiac Northern Senior High school at just about the time my dad was released from prison and through some creative financial meanderings my father bought a nice house in Waterford, Michigan and we settled in for a respectable summer. At least that is what I was hoping for.

The respectable summer turned out to be a nightmare as my mother came to live with us, even though my parents had been divorced years earlier. She brought our youngest brother with her and every day my parents fought like cats and dogs. The fighting seemed to escalate and then of course, the police were called. When they finally arrived, it was not good. My dad was an ex-felon, and my mom was in the living room crying. She kept telling the police that she just wanted to leave and take my younger brother with her but that my dad would not let her.

Now in my fragile mind, my mother was about to take my brother away from me again so as they talked, I asked my mom if I could take Jason outside and tell him goodbye. She gave me permission and they all stayed inside with the police.

I do not know what I was thinking, which happened a lot, but after talking to my little brother, I told him I had a plan. He was nine at the time and so we hopped over the fence, and I picked him up and we just started running. I had no shoes on nor did he, but I ran and ran and ran some more. My feet got all bloodied, I ran through the woods and eventually found this bait shop where I convinced the owner that we were in trouble.

I could only think of one person to call. Someone who was crazier than me, my Aunt Wanda. I called her and sure enough, she was off to the rescue. She sent my cousin; he picked us up and we went into hiding.

After a few days, my dad gave Jason back to my mom and they moved to Illinois, and we stayed in Michigan.

I got a job working for a guy who ran a chop shop (stole and sold illegal car parts) and then decided to enlist in the army and just get away from my father. I chose the army because I figured it was the quickest way away and I did not think my dad knew anyone in the army. I had tried to join the Navy as a Nuclear Engineer years earlier when I was still in Miami. I had even taken the first pledge and enlisted in the delayed entry program.

I probably would have gone but the recruiter ended up trying to seduce me for sex and that put the fear of God in him and in me. I wanted nothing to do with the Navy after that so when I threatened to go to the police, he found a way to let me get out.

I slipped out years later from my dad's and spent the night at a military recruiter's house in Detroit and the recruiter partied with me. We got drunk and then he dropped me off to enlist the next morning. I was sent down to the Ren-Cen in Detroit at the age of 18 and put up in a hotel room where all the recruits just sat around and played poker and drank. The next day I woke up heavily hung over and went through all the drills of signing up to enlist. I finally got a job as an MP in West Germany guarding missiles and was signing my life away on the dotted line (I was going to leave that day for boot camp) when I just panicked and asked the military people if I could have one more breath of freedom. They agreed, and I went outside and ran. (Yes, I did a lot of running from everyone and everything).

My military career lasted one day, then I went back to live with my dad and signed up for college. I had pretty good ACT scores so I figured I would go to the University of Detroit and study business. It was my goal to end up at Law School where I knew that I could make a lot of money legitimately working for some not so legitimate people.

During the couple of months of summer, I drank and did whatever I could to pass the time away but inside my life was growing rottener and I was growing more bitter and numb by the day, I know—hard to imagine right? The ugliness of my first 18 years were starting to permanently alter me and I knew that I was about to cross a line from which I might never return, the line of permanent damnation as I could feel within me the great desire to just walk away from hope and anything that might resemble anything good. I did not want to live, but the sad part was that I did not really care.

The highlight of that summer was an event that scared me like no other event up to that point and in hindsight was yet another attempt by God to grab my attention. It all started when my cousin and I met these two girls and ended up on a date. We scored tickets to the Lover Boy and Quiet Riot concert at the Pine Knob Amphitheater in Clarkston, Michigan and we were all excited about the evening. The only drag was that alcohol was not allowed and so we were bummed and kept trying to figure out ways that we could get around this small impediment.

I spent a couple of days trying to figure out a solution to this situation and eventually produced a novel idea. We bought this Styrofoam ice chest, two six packs of Coke and some chewing gum along with a few corks and then brought all of that stuff to my cousin's garage. Once there we drained out all the soda by punching a small hole in the bottom of one of the six packs of coke while leaving the other six pack alone.

After the six pack was emptied, we then got out a bottle of Jack Daniel's whiskey and proceeded to fill each of the emptied cans up with it. After we were done, we stuck in a cork and then chewed some gum and then used that chewed gum to form a seal around the cork. We then put the corked cans on the bottom of the cooler and put some ice in it and then placed the normal six pack on top and went off to the concert.

When we got to Pine Knob, the people checking the beverages reached into our cooler and pulled out the top six pack and saw that the bottom one was also Coke, so they did not bother to check it out, so we were in and so was our valuable contraband. I am pretty sure that the people around us thought we were losing our minds as we proceeded to get blitzed only from drinking Coke.

It did not take too long for us to get inebriated, and I can remember lying on the grass trying to grab the laser lights as they shot up overhead during the concert. The music was loud, the effects were great, and I was just chilling while trying to forget my woes.

After the concert I was elected to drive my cousin's big four-wheel drive truck home because I was the most sober of the bunch, which really was not saying much. What it really meant was that I was the one that was still able to move my hand to such a degree that I could put a key into the ignition. We all piled up in the truck, and I got it started up and with great concentration I somehow got us in line to leave the concert.

It was this big snake-like line, and everyone was in a hurry to get out of there but there was only one way in and only one way out. Everyone was doing their best to weasel in front of you and as we inched out way closer and closer to the exit my aggravation level with the crowds and vehicles was growing more intense.

We were only a few cars away from the first significant turn towards the exit when this little car in front of us started to play around with us. Most people in line were impatiently trying to go forward but this little two-seater in front of us was being driven by two girls and they took an entirely different tactic to pass the time. They put their little sports car into reverse and instead of going forward, they moved backwards and ended up tapping our front bumper and then they put it into drive and moved off a few feet and giggled and looked back at us.

I looked out the window to cuss them out and then the girls started flirting with us but instead of taking it for a compliment it really seemed to make me flat out mad. I could not imagine why this little car thought it could damage our truck, but that stupid little car was not giving up and put itself into reverse again. I knew it was prepping for another tap but this time I was going to surprise them.

I reached down and put the truck into low 4-wheel drive and determined that I was simply going to run them over if they did it again. I can still feel the adrenaline rush that came upon me as I prepared myself for some monster truck action. I gave the engine a little gas and as I stared down at the midget mobile, they started to go into reverse but just at that time the guy directing traffic in front of us waved us on.

I hit the gas with determination because I wanted to hit that little car a bit none the less but as the attendant waved me through the little sports car shot forward and even though I was aiming for it, I was left in the dust but had managed to get up quite a good head of steam. Since there was no little car to drive over in front of me the truck shot straight forward with no limits and as I started into the intersection a lady directly in front of me, perpendicular to the truck, opened her door and stepped out and at that moment I knew I was going to run her over.

I can still remember it as if it were yesterday. I threw up my hands and screamed, too drunk to let my foot off the accelerator, and the truck lunged forward and right before I plastered that poor lady on the street the truck turned left and then stopped. I suddenly was very sober and put my hands carefully back upon the wheel and I knew that an Angel had just reached down from heaven and saved me from a charge of murder.

I continued to drive to the home of the two girls where we crashed on the floor but on the way to their apartment complex, we were followed by a police cruiser and my new soberness really came in handy.

It was about three weeks later that I received a call from an admissions representative of Andrews University, a private Christian University in Southwestern Michigan, asking me if I wanted to enroll and I said there was no way that I could afford to do so. Andrews did not give up on me and worked it out and so within one week I was on my way to Andrews where I was planning on being a pre-law major. I had been offered a job working as a lawyer for the Sicilian mob with a starting salary of $1,000,000.

The lawyer had confided in me that I had been offered the job because of my dad and because they knew that I knew how to keep my mouth shut. It seemed like a good deal and so I ran off from my family (Andrews was on the other side of the State of Michigan, four hours away) thinking I was running away from God as well.

Boy was I wrong.

Chapter Twelve

It is ridiculous to imagine that one could run from God, but I was doing everything I could to do so. I had given up on the idea of running drugs myself but what could happen if I only defended drug dealers as their lawyer? It would be the best of both worlds and all I really needed was a college degree and then a quick trip to law school and I would be set.

I made the four-hour drive to Andrews University with my dad and uncle. I did not know anyone at the school and would have gone without much if it had not been for my Aunt Wanda who bought me some clean jeans, underwear, etc.... I was a minimalist at the time and really did not have much to my name.

I came onto the campus of Andrews University in the Fall of 1983 and received a room in Meier Hall and was assigned a roommate from central Ohio by the name of Don. Don was an accountant type of guy but one that was a good friend by the time our four years were over.

When I arrived at Andrews, I had to go through first-year students' orientation and it was during that time of getting acquainted with Andrews that I met a man from Oregon, named Jamie. Jamie was an older student and one that was on fire for God. He and I became friends and I learned that his father had ties to the mob on the west coast. I secretly wondered if he was there to spy on me and he was wondering the same thing but for whatever reason we became friends and everywhere he went, I went and everywhere I went, he went.

We hung out together all through the orientation time and as we progressed through that time, we had ample time to talk. We talked about life in the mob, about our dad's, about God and about how God had kept us alive, in spite of us. I did not mind talking about life in the mob or even my dad, but I really was uncomfortable talking about God.

Deep down I knew that God had supernaturally protected me and had called me into ministry as a tenth grader, but I really wanted to forget about all of that. I knew that God was real because I could clearly remember back when I was eight years old, and my cousin and brother and I all saw an evil face appear in the sky when we lived in Ortonville. I knew that evil existed, but I truly hoped that if I left evil alone it would leave me alone.

During freshman orientation, God and Jamie would not leave me alone. He kept reminding me of the times I should have crashed, of the times I was shot at and lived, and how God had repeatedly put His hand upon me to spare my life. I did not want to hear it but as he talked, I grew convicted and started to see that God had secretly tricked me into coming to a Christian University.

It was the night before we were to register for school, and we stayed up late into the night and he lectured and kept hammering me over God's providence in my life. Over and over Jamie kept telling me that the only reason I was alive was that God had called me into the Gospel ministry and I could feel myself being drawn to that choice but if there was one thing that I never wanted to be it was a minister.

When I thought of ministers, I always heard the conversations my family had about them and how bad they all seemed to be. I can remember telling people that the last thing I would ever be was a pastor. I mean, my family were the people who set the alarms on their watches to ring with some loud annoying song at noon, just so that the minister would know it was time to wrap things up. My family were the ones who wore ties with naked ladies on the back and then flipped them up at opportune moments to distract the minister during the sermon. My family really did not care about God, church was just this social hangout place. The minister was not some holy dude, he was simply a mark. At one point my cousin tried to encourage me to plant some cocaine behind the license plate of our minister so that we could turn him in to the police.

We would arrive at church in a limo or a corvette or some fancy thing and the church was comprised by about 1/3 of my family members. I felt bad for the minister...I never wanted to be the minister.

Well, after talking to Jamie I knew my worst nightmare was true and so I signed up the next morning as a reluctant Religion major. I guess I should have not been surprised because I clearly remembered that day back in 10th grade when I was walking to play football on a Saturday morning and as I neared the fence where we were going to play, I heard someone say, "You are going to be a minister." It was loud and clear, and I know there was no mistaking it. I even called the local church and told them about the experience, but I am sure they also thought that I was out of my mind.

The day of registration I declared my major as Pre-Seminary, which meant my entire goal was to get to the Seminary where I would be trained to be a minister. You would have thought that I would have been excited now that I knew I was living the life God had called me to, but it was not like that at all. Instead of being elated I was miserable.

I knew how rotten a person I really was and somehow, I got the idea into my head that I was going to have to do penance to get right with God, even if I did not love Him. I was fully aware that God existed and that I would work for Him, but it did not mean that I had to like it. I just needed some rules to live by and so I set about trying to figure out the rules.

My idea of God said that I had to prevent myself from sinning or God would reach down from heaven and send a lightning bolt to get my attention. I was paranoid of sin, and I can remember going to the Mishawaka Mall after a couple of months of college and going into the mall determined to not sin. I found a seat in the middle of the mall and looked down at the floor because I knew that if I were to look up and see a girl and have any evil thought in my mind, it would be sin and God would "get me."

I was terrified. One night I was walking to the dorm from a late night out and right in front of the dorm I stopped. It was raining and there was some lightning in the distance and I started yelling at God to leave me alone. I was so mad at Him for calling me as a minister, for the unfair demands that He had placed upon my life. I wanted freedom from Him, I wanted to live life on my own terms, but I was deeply terrified to even attempt to do so.

God, that rotten being in the sky, had trapped me and I did not like it one bit. As a result, I fought hard and consistently with God. Every quarter I changed my major to something else only to go back to the Religion major thing after flirting with other choices such as architecture, business, physical education and pretty much any and every other option as well. Each time I returned to my religion major because I was deathly afraid that I would be condemned by God if I didn't. I could handle the condemnation, but I could not handle what I thought came with it, namely an all-out attack by God. I believed God was ruthless and the thought that He might love me never entered my mind.

After my first quarter at Andrews University, I went home without really knowing if I was ever going to go back to college or not. I had barely passed with a low "C" average and my attempt at following the rules was not going well. I did not know what I wanted to do at the time but the day I was leaving college to go home, the pastor of our church, Dwight Nelson, called me up because he said God had put me on his heart. He encouraged me and then let me go stating that he was excited about what God was going to do in my life in the new year.

I hung up on him and cussed out God quietly, "leave me alone."

I went back home for the break and needed to make some cash so I started hanging out with my cousin who was busy restoring a corvette, which he said I could help him with for some spending money. I would spend my time working on that car and attempting to get high off the paint fumes. As I did so the struggle with what was going on inside of me was overwhelming at times. I could feel Satan trying to push me away from anything righteous and my mind was like a motion picture of the past complete with scenes that I never wanted to remember.

It was as if Satan was trying to get me to believe that I was worthless, had no hope and was beyond the help of God. It only took about a week for me to cave in under the pressure and late one night I opened the bottom drawer of my cousin's tool chest and lifted out the sacred and familiar bottle of Jack Daniel's. That was all it took, and I surrendered and decided to skip going back to school.

When the Christmas break was nearing its end, I informed my family that I was just going to stay home but my aunt, who I feared more than my dad, got in my face, and told me that I was going back to school. For some reason she planted a fear deep within my bones and I actually listened to her and made the trek back to Andrews University for yet another quarter of school.

In hindsight, I am glad that my aunt forced me back to college but finishing that year was quite difficult. I had to fight for sanity, for the desire to attend church and stay sober. I continued to change my major away from Pre-Seminary and felt haunted by a God that I did not want to serve but was afraid to "not."

As the school year came to a close, I was forced to consider what I was going to do for the summer. The previous summer I had been working with stolen cars and doing hay with my cousins but this summer I wanted to try something different. Because I was a religion guy who was officially signed up to be a minister I was encouraged to try selling religious books door to door.

It seemed as though anyone who desired to be a minister for my denomination was encouraged, almost expected, to sell religious books door to door. These people were called "Literature Evangelists," and so I figured if I was going to be a minister I might as well do my time selling books.

I looked around and then settled in on a summer job selling religious books in Detroit. I was to be a Literature Evangelist and so my uncle loaned me a car, a 1972 pea green Pontiac Catalina with no air conditioning, and I worked trying to sell books in the worst part of the inner city.

My job entailed carrying this large leather looking book bag from door to door and trying to get people to let me into their house. Once inside I would set up my little backdrop, which folded into my case, and then would spin my tale of how these books would transform their lives. I really was a terrible salesperson as I wanted to give away the books more than sell them.

I did not manage to sell much that summer but did grow empathy for all postal employees as I had some pretty good encounters with mad dogs chasing me. It was a good way to stay in shape as at least once a week I was forced to run as fast as I could from some unwelcoming dog. My worst encounter involved me jumping up onto my car with the briefcase in front of me as Cujo tried to eat me alive.

Overall, I survived the summer but working as a Literature Evangelist did not really help my faith much. I am not sure if it was because I really did not want to do it or if it had more to do with living with my dad and brothers at the time. My dad was out on parole, and we were all living in a nice house. We "played" house together and tried to look like a presentable lot, but it was tough.

My dad would always start off nice when he got out of prison or jail. He would embrace jailhouse religion when he was inside and that determination to serve God would last about six months and slowly, he would morph back to some evil dude. My first time back home after college was right at the time he was starting to revert and as a result, unfortunately, I walked in on him one day when he was drunk with a 9mm pistol in his hand.

I came home from work early that day and walked into the living room where I found my dad sitting on the floor by a chair. He was forlorn and distraught and had his Baretta in his hand spinning it in a circle. When I saw him, I knew that I should back away but before I could he locked eyes with me and told me to come in and sit down. I did not think I had much of a choice at the time, so I came in and sat down in the chair. He proceeded to pour out through drunken tears how disappointed he was in me and how he felt as though I judged him for living life the way he had lived it.

He kept pointing the gun at me and it did not take too long for me to realize that I was going to die. I was totally paralyzed and could not move from the chair. I was frozen and all emotion evaporated from my body. I think I was in shock because the longer he talked and the more he spun the gun and pointed it at me off and on the more I just checked out.

The spell that he wove that day was broken when the pistol went off and as he pointed it at me, he fired repeatedly and miraculously, not a single shot hit me. After the gun was empty my dad looked at me and simply said, "I guess you are going to call the cops now." He then got up and walked away and I collapsed on the floor terrified.

There was no way I was going to call the cops as I knew that my dad would kill me if I did that. I knew that my dad could reach out for me even if he was in prison and I was not about to get on his bad side, at least any worse than I already had.

The summer continued after that and as it did, I found myself looking forward to going back to school but not because I wanted to learn, rather it was an acceptable escape from my insane father, who was growing more evil by the moment.

While I finished up my last month of summer work, I also discovered something else about our home. It was haunted. I do not mean like one of those reality tv show type of hauntings but there were creepy things happening. Shadows would move around, an ice-cold presence would emerge, my brother saw things, and you could "feel" evil. It was terrifying and I wanted out of there so badly.

When I did escape from that house I never went back there. My dad eventually moved and from that point onward I only went back to visit my dad for a day or two but never stayed with him longer than that. My trust for him was gone and I knew it was courting death and evil to be around him.

Eventually my summer of Halloween ended, and my fright night experience was left behind and I ran off to college. I went back as a Pre-seminary major and became a legalistic jerk. I had been so scared the previous summer that I went about trying to save everyone from the clutches of hell and it did not matter that I had no relationship with God because I thought you just needed to live like you did and everything would be taken care of.

I guess I was trying to get people to receive the "get out of hell free card" and it never dawned upon me that you would actually have to have a relationship with Jesus Christ. The concept of a loving God was foreign to me.

I became the symbol of the perfect hypocrite. I preached righteousness and since I was a fairly good communicator, I even started going out preaching at area churches. The problem was that I was preaching on the strength of my own personality. I did not want anything to do with God but because I felt as though God was forcing me to serve him, I figured I would live however I wanted as long as I served him as a minister.

I became a legalistic pain in the butt, at least on the outside. My fear of God had transformed me into someone who went around scaring everyone else into becoming a Christian. I was full of brimstones and fire towards everyone else but of course, at the same time, I was fooling around with my girlfriend. I was such a hypocrite that I even talked about how everyone else was a hypocrite. I even had one friend tell me that I was the perfect budding minister, I thought, "If they only knew." I would proclaim a life of purity and holiness while at the same time living a life of sin and debauchery. I had perfected the outward appearance but inside was mostly rotten. My mental, physical and sexual abuse had imprinted upon my psyche and the person I became was one that was extremely wounded.

Chapter Thirteen

I am not sure how it all came to be but, in my heart, I had somehow transferred my fear of my father over to God and I started looking at God as if He was the enemy and if I ever got out of line, then wham...He would smite me. God was some sort of mythical Thor like being who acted more like Loki. He lived in the heavens and went around carrying lightning bolts for the purpose of using those bolts to zap those who got out of line.

It did not help that I got into a relationship with a girl whose father worked for the denomination that I was a part of as a high-level executive. He was a wonderful man who desired to be the father I had never known. He took me under his wing and proceeded to buy me clothes and teach me how to act. I lost my identity and started taking on his and through our relationship he taught me about all that was wrong with my denomination. He would tell me when some great leader would have a cardinal fall and how the denomination would cover it up. He shared with me all the negative and as I result, I started seeing the denomination as a negative thing as well.

My relationship with his daughter proved to be an up and down affair. We got too close physically and then the guilt would kick in and we would break up. On one occasion her father came to me and told me to trust him. He said that I needed to marry his daughter because she was what I needed. I took him at his word and so we got married after I graduated from college.

Our two-week honeymoon proved to be a disaster and no matter what we did it just seemed as though we could not get along. We could not even consummate our marriage because of health reasons and the frustration of that perfect marriage shattered and just got stuffed deeper inside my mind. We got through the honeymoon in North Carolina and ended up heading back to Michigan where we moved into an apartment so that I could go to work as an assistant pastor in Detroit and she could, well, what she did was go back to her parents and then go back to school for the summer.

We spent the majority of time apart and the senior pastor who I worked under told me that he did not even know I was coming to work for him until I called him up. As a matter of fact, our first official meeting was at a Big Boy's, and I can clearly remember him sitting across from me and in that conversation, he told me that I was "not called into the ministry." Our relationship only went down from there. I was the young whipper snapper who supposedly was after his job, and he was the old salesman who had gotten into ministry through the back door with no education.

And that was one of the best things about my life! I was alone in my apartment, the assistant minister of two churches, working for a pastor who hated me, and I felt as though I could not trust a sole, including and especially God. Somehow it was as though God had cursed me and I could picture Him up in heaven pulling the strings of my puppet life and laughing. The years of doubt, low self-esteem, abuse, and everything did a work on me. I am not sure what impacted me more than anything else.

I had no identity and was as messed up as one could be. Even now, looking back on the first 23 years of my life is so depressing. How could one go through so much and still be alive? It probably would have been merciful for God to just let me die but for some reason He kept me alive. Every part of my heart had been infiltrated with evil and disappointment and I was numb and in a fog.

On the outside, I was a pastor who publicly lived this awesome life, complete with wingtips and a nice suit, but internally I was a more than a mess. I found myself identifying with psychopaths because I really did not care about people. There was a deadness to my inner spirit and if I were going through that today I am sure I would have taken some blade or razor and started cutting on my arm to "feel alive."

The deadness permeated my existence, and I sought some reprieve in pornography. I hated the church, hated being a minister, feared God and yet I was cocky. I thought I was God's gift to the church because I was such a great speaker and would be told by people that I was this great evangelist.

My veneer lasted less than a year and then I quit. I moved to Lansing to attend Law School and pretty much self-destructed. When I graduated college, I was full of promise, a budding star in the denomination. A year later I was divorced and in law school trying to run from God as best I could.

However, God would not leave me alone. I tried to run as far from Him as I could, but I had this nagging deep within me that kept me from being satisfied. I hated God but viewed Him with that rotten lightning bolt and knew that I had to serve Him or be fried. I was a slave with no free will

While I was in the law school, we would all head off to the local bar each Friday after school to let off steam. I would watch respectful lawyers and judges became idiots under the influence and it seemed as though everyone around me was getting blitzed, cheating on their wives, or actually having sex in the back of the bar. I could feel God telling me to get out, but I did not know what else to do.

My confusion lasted for two semesters and then out of frustration I left school and went back to Andrews University where I enrolled, of all places, into the Theological Seminary to once again study to be a minister. I was a glutton for punishment who pretty much had no backbone when it came to God. I did not want to be a minister, but I now knew that I did not have a choice. My destiny was set and the evil emperor, God in my case, was forcing me to do His beckon will.

I realized that as much as I despised God, I needed Him. I was going to be really evil, or I was going to have to fight to be really good. There was no middle ground for me, and I could feel the blood flowing through me of my past and if I ever let it get out, it just would not be good.

I had no personal relationship with God, hated him actually, had no devotional life, only picked up my Bible when I had to for school, and was living a life of debauchery whenever I could. I ended up having a fling with a lifeguard, getting drunk on occasion, and finding myself losing my soul in the process. In my mind I was obeying God. He might have forced me to go to school, but he was not going to change me. I figured I would do his thing for him and then live any way I wanted for me. It was my compromise, and he would just have to live with it. Like it or not.

However, God did not play fair. By the Fall I was content in my hypocrisy and was also involved in the intramural flag football program at the college. I was playing with a team of people I knew, and I was also still in rather good shape, and I was especially fast!

One of our first games, my team put me on the line to rush the quarterback because of my speed and the other defensive end on our team was Curt, who was also fast. Upon the snapping of the ball both Curt and I went all out and as we went down to reach for the flag of the quarterback to sack him, the quarterback stepped up and Curt and I collided. The top of his head hit my right orbit and we both collapsed as if we had been shot.

I was dizzy and groggy and thought I had a concussion. I did not feel so good but thought that overall, I was doing fine. I stayed and watched part of the game and then headed back to my apartment. I can remember sitting on the couch when a friend came over and looked all concerned. I said I was all right, and they said that I should go to the hospital. I refused but then they asked me to do a favor. They told me to put one hand on one side of my face and then put my other hand on the other side.

Upon doing this I immediately realized that the right side of my face was pushed in like an inch. It took all of my strength not to panic but I did agree to head to the hospital where they admitted me and scheduled me for surgery the next morning. They told me that my right orbit was crushed, and they were going to have to go in and rebuild it.

I was not a happy camper and instantly I knew that this was God's revenge. I had dared to stand up to him and this was how he was getting me back. I hated, hated, hated him (did I tell you that I hated Him?). I cussed him out and if I could have gotten my hands on him, well... You get the idea.

All night long as I was stuck in that hospital bed I vented my anger towards God. I saw my life for the total mess that it was, and I knew it was because God was playing with me like some pissy chess game. I felt rage deep within and I wanted out. I battled throughout the night and was still intent on being stubborn until I was startled by my early morning visitor.

It was early in the morning when the anesthesiologist came by and had me sign some papers releasing the hospital from all liability if I died, that I realized the seriousness of my situation. Yes, I was mad at God, but I had been taught about hell for those who were not righteous and when the subject of death came up all of a sudden, I could see myself heading directly for hell without stopping to collect $200 at Go. I sure did not want to go there so I was really stuck. As I read over the papers and signed my name, I was never so afraid. I did not want to die; hell was not an enjoyable thought, but neither was being a Christian for a God who I could not trust and who seemed intent on destroying me by allowing every sort of crappy thing to impact me.

Before I was taken into surgery the chaplain of the hospital came to pray with me, but I did not want him to say a word. The idea that God cared for me or that He would make anything easier on me was not a possibility in my mind. I just wanted Him to leave me alone and keep me out of hell, if hell really existed.

I was released from the hospital after surgery and went back to the duplex that I was renting at the time. Because of my accident, my right eye was severely affected, and the seal of the eye lid was not right and so my right eye would tear up at the strangest times and the result was that I could not see out of that eye with much clarity.

I tried working at various jobs but ended up unemployed, living in a small basement apartment, drinking alcohol, and life became escaping creditors and watching the Late Show with David Letterman and yet still I thought I was beating God at his own game. I had somehow found a way to dodge His cruel demand of me and so I just wasted my life and laughed in his face.

Yet I was miserable and just did not know what to do.

Years ago, I had heard Chuck Swindoll say, "God takes impossible people, breaks them down until they cannot go any farther, and then calls them to a task that only they can do." I was finally near to that point, or so I thought, and as I sank lower and lower, I tried to call out to God but was afraid that I was too far gone.

I was beyond hopeless and pretty sure that I had committed the unforgiveable sin, but I hated where I was at, so I was desperate to try anything, including God.

Dan Allender in his book, "Healing the Wounded Heart," wrote:

Evil knows that to the degree we are discouraged and defeated; we will not fight for survival. To not fight is to capitulate, to surrender. Evil does not primarily want to kill us; instead, it wants us to spend our lives in worry or regret. Its design is to take life from life, or in other words, to kill hope. It loves for us to sour ourselves through ruminating on failure and obsessing over the disasters we anticipate in the future. Both regret and worry sap creativity and plunge the heart into the slough of despair.

Evil has a way of distorting all things and painting an emotional picture that seems bleak. When I was in that place it seemed as though the past was dictating my future and that there was no escape. Whether it was when I went to sleep and could only fixate on the negative, inner critic in my head or when I was trying to move forward and hit roadblock and after roadblock.

Satan likes to slip in and whisper, "there is no hope for you."

It is a powerful lie but one that seems extremely true. What is the voice in your head? What is the past that you believe you cannot escape? How many times have you failed and have you reached the helplessness state where you have hit zombie status?

The truth is that God never gives up and that He always seeks to connect with us. I have heard it said that God is the God of second chances, but nothing could be further from the truth. God is the God of infinite chances. No matter how many times we have failed He will always reach down and pull us up "again." Get it in your head that God will never give up on you, so you do not give up on you either.

Chapter Fourteen

Somehow in the midst of my downward and depressed state I had a revelation and knew that if I was going to shake myself from my slumber I was going to have to reach down and grab life by its bootstraps. My father was always the person who said you have to try harder. He always made it a point that no matter how hard I tried that I would not succeed but he did model an attitude of never giving up.

I took that toxic belief and inserted it into my mind and made the choice to break my pattern of self-destruction and immediately my willpower was set. I simply built a wall from my past, from all that needed to be processed and internalized it all. I told myself that nothing before now mattered so I could do it and move forward and that my past would not influence me moving forward.

I started behaving as any believer would, or so I thought. I started attending church, reading my Bible, attempting to pray, and from the outside looking as if I had it all together. I still did not understand the human psyche and the way trauma impacts us moving forward into the future and I really thought the way to have success was to ignore all the negative in life. I took out my mason tools and built a brick wall around me to keep me from having to deal with all the crap.

My relationship with God was one birthed out of necessity, fear, desperation, and loneliness. I returned to Andrews University and over the next two years earned my Master's degree in Educational and Developmental Psychology. As part of that degree, I earned enough credits to become eligible to become a counselor and I also took several graduate level classes at the Seminary. I knew that I was called into ministry, but I still acted like a thoroughbred with a bit in their mouth chafing at the restrictions.

There is a lot of power in a false perception of God. I had never met anyone who I thought 'loved' Jesus, so it was hard to imagine that it was even possible. What made life even worse is that when I was born there was so much trauma in my life that my ability to bond was not that great. I knew how to act and went about doing what I could, but I did not "feel" many of the things people told me they felt. I had relationships but never felt the depth of love that some described, I had friends but was a loner deep in my heart, and the damage done to my DNA—my core—was beyond any that you could imagine

But I was on my way to cognitive sainthood and was feeling "intellectually" good. If Martin Luther could lock himself in a cave and beat himself with whips, then I could force myself into a great relationship with God as well. (Yes, my mind actually thought that). My works were lining up with where they should be, and I learned all about the Bible. I had Old Testament theology classes, New Testament theology classes, Hermeneutics, Greek, Hebrew and by the time I was graduating with my master's degree I had learned some great counseling skills and was now an esteemed expert on the Bible. I was starting to feel like I was saved or at least good enough to get in.

Sigmund Freud espoused an explanation for the human psyche. He said that a person was like a house with an attic, main level, and a basement. The attic was the best part of the mind. It was where all the good thoughts and desires were kept. The very best of us, the part that if we won a billion dollars, we would go to some third world country and give it all away and possibly die from true sacrifice. The basement was full of spider webs, chain saws and bad thoughts and the main part of the house was what people saw, which in reality was the balance between the attic and the basement.

All of my past was in the basement of my mind and so I did what any red-blooded male (in denial) would do—I bolted and locked the door and tried like crazy to keep all of the evil from leaking out. All the garbage from my past, all the abuse, all the uncertainty, my temper and anger...you name it, I cracked open the basement door and tossed it in while kicking back the other stuff so it would not escape.

I really thought that I could keep things at bay, so I gave it a valiant effort. I started exercising, moved to an apartment on the campus of my college, started reorienting my thoughts back to being a minister, and life looked like it had finally turned a corner. I started doing what others had said was important to do. The thing I was missing?

Jesus.

Chapter Fifteen

It took me two years to finish my master's degree and at times it did not seem like I was going to be able to make it. I had this thing that if a teacher were teaching me something from the book that I would challenge them and that "spirit" or "ego" within me made me appear to be a jerk. I do not know why it was so hard for me to simply extend grace, but I had to make everything difficult.

When the completion of my time at Andrews was drawing to a close, I had to start thinking what I was going to do for my career. I had a couple of choices. I could continue down my quest of becoming a minister for the denomination or I could pivot and enroll into the Doctor of Psychology program and focus on becoming a psychologist. I was wrestling with the possibilities with another choice presented itself. I was offered a position to move to Georgia and work with the Fund-Raising Program of a small community hospital. One of the jobs I had at Andrews while as a student was helping faculty obtain grants for special programs. This inadvertently put me into a place where I got to know some individuals who did fundraising for hospitals and when they heard I was graduating, their interest was piqued.

While I was trying to figure out the future, my other boss, Herdley, (yes, I had another job) who worked for the Guidance and Testing department asked if I could stop by her office. I had been working with her in developing a Peer Helper network at the school. We had created a room on the lower level of Nethery Hall where students could hang out if they were emotionally challenged, feeling overwhelmed or were just battling with an addiction of any kind. It was a new type of program, and I geared the advertising to play off of a popular movie at the time, Ghostbusters. I made these posters that said, "You were you going to call?" Peer Helpers!

I helped train volunteer students and it turned out to be a successful program for the school. I spent a great deal of time with Herdley developing it and as a result, she had gotten to know me fairly well.

I can still remember our meeting. She graciously waded into my life and asked me a question, "Pat, do you think you have an anger problem?"

Now, as you are probably aware, there is no "good" way to ask someone if they have an anger problem. I was totally in denial and so when she asked, I immediately "blew up." I got angry, upset, and challenged her. "How could she believe such a thing?" She did the best she could to de-escalate my temper, but I left that meeting thinking that she really did not know me at all.

Anger is a secondary emotion that we use to cover up the primary emotion that was triggered. Anger is not the first response, it is hurt, loneliness or disappointment or such things like that. Anger is the tool we use to protect ourselves from those feelings and we can only get angry if we personalize what it is that is being said or done. We have to have this mental game playing in our head that says, "How dare you think that of ME." It has to be personalized for me to use the anger tool.

Anger usually is related to an event or thought and then passes fairly quickly. I did not have an anger problem. I had a rage problem. Rage is anger bottled up over time that just brews and builds. It is like going around as the Incredible Hulk so that if anyone does anything that startles me, upsets me, impacts me, I react. That little scratch on the surface allows the lava of putrid, hot rage to pour out always in excess of the trigger.

Growing up I witnessed firsthand the rage of my father, and his training found its mark. I learned whoever had the biggest stick wins. I tried not to resort to physical violence, but I had mastered the art of hurtful words and looks. I would manipulate, make people feel small or belittled and I would use my knowledge to overwhelm and intimidate.

Herdley had witnessed the rage lashing out and she did her best to help tamper it down but even though I had tried going to counseling I just couldn't be real with myself. That self-awareness thing was beyond my reach and even though one of my professors had tried to get all of her students to visualize a better version of who we were in the future, it still was a struggle.

My vision board that I had created was simple. I had thought about who I wanted to be in the future and the only calm person I could identify was Mr. Rogers from PBS Television. He would walk into his house, change his sweater and shoes and project this amazing calm. I wanted to be like that guy and so on my vision board there was a picture of Mr. Rogers, a Cracker Barrel type rocking chair, a guy smoking a pipe, a porch overlooking some relaxing woods and a lake. It seemed like a great image of calm and wisdom. That was my goal but let us just say I was struggling to reach it.

As my future plans were rolling around there was a job fair held in the Student Center where opportunities to serve as a missionary emerged. The Japan Union of our denomination sent a representative to Andrews to gather college age folk who were interested in serving on the mission field in Japan. Pastor Kim was the one that had been dispatched and he came to Andrews to recruit students to come serve in Japan.

I was curious about the possibilities and so I went to talk with Pastor Kim, and he eventually offered me a Position in Japan where I would be working at the Chiba English Language Institute and as part of the deal, I was going to be able to start an English-speaking church at the school. I had always thought missionaries had a higher level of spirituality and so it appealed to me to make a bigger difference for God. I mean what better way to earn points for heaven?

I accepted the position knowing nothing about being a missionary. I was from Detroit however, so I did know a bit about Japan. In Detroit, which was the headquarters for the big three United States auto makers, the nation of Japan was a threat and not looked upon positively. Japan was making big inroads in the automotive market and Honda; Mazda and Toyota were looked at as the enemy. I thought if anyone needed God, it would have to be the savages of Japan.

The future looked great, I was a missionary, was going to be able to plant a church and they were going to provide an apartment, help get transportation to Japan, move all my stuff and would not have to worry about any expenses. It seemed like a wonderful opportunity, or at least that is what I kept telling myself.

When the time came to finally pack up and leave for Japan, I was less optimistic. The week before I was to leave, I had pretty much changed my mind and fear had gripped me and thinking about going to another country had become overwhelming. My anxiety returned to higher levels and my stomach, nerves, bowels and thoughts all ended up swirling around all of the time. I was actually going to turn down the job, but I had a dream. In the dream I had turned down the job and like Jonah, instead of flying towards Japan, I got on a plane and flew the other way.

God spoke to me in the dream, and I knew I was running away so because I did not want to do anything to displease God, I caved and continued with the quest of becoming a mighty missionary of faith.

On the way to the airport to fly to Japan my dad had come up to say goodbye and on the way to the airport my nerves totally collapsed, and we had to stop at every rest stop to take a bathroom break. It was so bad that when we got to the airport I was curled up in a ball and they put me in a wheelchair. Here I was, this great missionary, heading to Japan to save the world, but I could not even stand up straight.

I forced myself to get on the airplane and I sat down and flew the 14 hours to Japan. When I arrived, it was like entering a new world. The moment I got to Narita Airport the words were all in Japanese and the spelling was different. Characters, letters that I was unfamiliar with and there was no internet or smart phones to help. I made my way through customs and all I could see was this huge wall of glass with a white coating. I figured if customs let me through, my last chance to run was before I got through the glass. I knew that people were there to greet me and take me to my house, but it took great concentration to simply put one foot in front of the other.

My years in Japan started when I walked through the doors and as I did, I was greeted by some officials from the Japan Union Mission. In their limited English they took me to where I was to be staying and when they pulled up to this tiny little house, I could feel that something was different. Pastor Kim came out to greet me and as best he could, he explained that I would be staying in his guest room until an apartment, which they called a "Manse" or mansion would be ready.

I was not happy about that as my room was a small empty space. A rolled-up mattress type of thing was my bed and I had to unroll it for night and then in the day, roll it back up and put it in this large shelf like holding area so that it could be used for other things during the day. But that was not the worst of it.

I was shown the bathroom, and it was like nothing I had ever seen. It was just a little bit bigger than the airplane bathroom and there was no toilet. The room was coated with a rubber-like surface, and I was told that to take a shower, I had to sit on a ridiculously small stool next to this tank like thing. I would use this little hose to wash off and then water would be placed in the tank like thing, heated by a propane heater and I was to get into that water, which then rose to my neck, and soak.

This was important because there was no central heating in the house, and it was January when I got there and so it was rather cold. They told me that if I sat in the hot water for about 30 minutes my body temperature would heat up and keep me warm for hours. Thus, I would not need a heater of any kind. I had no words but still was baffled by how to go to the bathroom.

My next instructions involved toilet use. They did not have toilets, at least not like anything I had ever used. Instead, there was a hole in the floor that had a ceramic ring around it, shaped oblong and you were to squat over it and do your business. All I could think of was how in the world could this be done, and I learned that if you squatted in the wrong direction anything that came out of you would miss.

That would have been a good talking point, but I guess they just assumed I could figure that part out, which after missing once, I did. But I was not happy about it.

Nothing was like it was supposed to be.

I had no idea what the food was before me, I could not understand the language, the Gulf War had just officially broken out and the people of Japan were protesting the United States involvement in it, and I stayed up late listening to Armed Forces Radio to catch up on the news of the war. I found myself attempting to eat at McDonald's and or Dunkin Donuts so that I could at least find something that reminded me of the good old USA. I was deep into culture shock and had no idea how to function but around anyone in Japan, I dug down deep and did my best to put on my happy face.

I eventually ended up living in a small apartment and my nerves were on the brink of total breakdown. Every night I would experience a panic attack and my coping skills involved sitting up rocking until my stomach stopped churning. I would translate the Celsius reading to Fahrenheit all night long on the small gas heater and just try to keep from being sick. I lost a lot of weight, could not hold anything down and in the midst of it...the church thing did not work out. Instead, I had to ride the train to a church in Chiba where nothing was understandable. I felt like a token you showed off. Look at the cool foreigner who works for us.

I did not like the culture, missed my family, and within just a couple of months the rock in my life, my Granny, died and I flew back to do her funeral.

While I was back in the States, I found out my dad had married a terrible lady that reminded me of Cruella Devil from the Disney Dalmation movies. She was as evil as a person that I could have ever imagined and just being around her gave me the creeps. As a matter of fact, many people in my family believed that the reason my Granny died was because this lady had placed a pillow over her face and suffocated her. She was a former model and con artist who had been in and out of prison. All she wanted was money and my dad seemed to be oblivious to her ways.

An autopsy was never done on my Granny and most just assumed she died in her sleep. The lady my dad married, Joelle, was jealous of my Granny and sought to pull dad away no matter what. I did not want anything to do with her, but she came along with us as we headed off from Michigan to Missouri to do the funeral.

I had been asked to do the funeral in Forsyth, Missouri for Granny and I tried not to let anything distract me. Although, in order to spend any time with my dad I had to hang out with him at some bar. I did manage to drink a Sprite regularly but just being in that environment was a nerve-racking place to be because when my dad got drunk, he got belligerent (he could be belligerent any time actually) and I just knew that a fight was going to break out at any moment. There would always be the threat of a fight and going to grab a Sprite meant that I was open to fighting just to save the family's honor.

Right before the funeral I was able to take my dad to see his cousin and of course the meetup was in a bar in downtown Detroit. My dad went in, and I reluctantly tagged along. We ended up sitting around this large table that could seat about 15 people and it was all full. My dad was near my cousin, who was a cop, at one end of the table and I was sitting at the other end just trying to sip my Sprite without arousing any suspicion and hoping that no one was about to get into a drunken brawl.

We were not there for too long when this strange looking woman walked up with long stringy hair and a look that said she was on heroin or some other mind-altering concoction. She introduced herself as a psychic and I did not know if she was or not, but she gave me the creeps.

She started reading palms and the first person she read was my cousin's palm, he was a cop, and she did not have anything good to say. She then went up to my father and he offered his palm and once again she only had evil things to report and summed it up by saying death was near.

Then she looked down at me and I looked away. She said, "hey, what about you?" I did not say anything but attempted to ignore her. She boldly said she wanted to read my palm and I just gave her a look that said, "don't even breathe my way." She was persistent and started coming towards my end of the table until my inebriated cousin, the Detroit cop, yelled some cuss words at her and said, "Hey, he works for the other guy." (My paraphrase, of course). She was too startled to speak and turned and walked away. I was in awe. I could not believe my cousin defended me or that he knew the side I represented.

I survived my remaining time there and then I got out of there as fast as I could and when I got back to Japan my stress intensified. I was not able to sleep much, and each night found me sitting up wrapping my arms around my legs as my nerves just went out. At this point, the rage and anger that had been building up within my life reached its climax and one night at the English Language School Pastor Kim attempted to confront me about my attitude, as my smile had long left me by that time, and I almost got into a fistfight with Pastor Kim. He was about 5 feet tall, brash, but I knew that I could take him. With my hands balled up into fists I could hear my brain saying, "don't do it," but I wanted to lash out in revenge. Instead, God once again intervened, and I ended up storming out of the office while saying a few choice words.

The mission could see that there was too much tension between us so their way of dealing with it was to promote me. Yep, for real. They asked me to transfer to the Japan Union College and be a professor there. I could teach English, conduct Business classes in the community and preach at the largest church in Japan that our denomination ran.

I became a Professor of Communication and I moved to the village of Otaki, which was in the center of the Bosu peninsula, about two hours from Tokyo. It was surrounded by rice fields and hills and was actually very beautiful. For those of you who do not know, the majority of the population in Japan live in the cities and they are packed tight but around the cities are these huge areas of beautiful mountains and fields. Otaki was an oasis and when I moved there, I got a bigger apartment, bought a car, and tried to make the best of things.

By the way, if you ever find yourself living in Japan do not buy a car. It is the Western way of doing things as it represented freedom, but the roads were tiny, the speed limit was low and the one time I tried to drive through Tokyo, people were walking faster than I could drive. It took forever and I never did that again. The train is by far the best way to get around and if you live in the city, just get a bike as everyone seems to have one.

The new digs gave me a bolt of adrenaline and as I adjusted to being a "professor," it fed my warped ego. Now I was a great missionary and a professor, and everyone looked up at me and the students, thought that I was so cool. But once again my earlier trauma was keeping me in an ever-vigilant mode and since I did not understand the language and it took great concentration to function in public without getting lost, my energy went into keeping myself calm.

I started running five miles in the morning and doing my best to get that energy out so that I could sleep. I was as thin as a person could get and tried to learn the language but everywhere I went people wanted to speak English so that they could practice.

I can remember thinking about what I had gotten into. It was tough enough navigating life in the States but now in a foreign country with no connections to anyone. It was a threat. I tried to handle the stress the best way possible. I even bought a television at one point but If I turned the television on it was Japanese television and every show was a weird game show or an old US movie that was dubbed in Japanese.

My entertainment became trying to learn to play tennis and listening to the Armed Forces Radio which would have news, radio programs and some National Football Games from the States in English.

I reluctantly did my job. I taught, preached, held some evangelistic meetings, and struggled with religion and the whole concept of God. It was during this time that I also started officially questioning my denomination's beliefs. When I had flown over to do my grandmother's funeral it had been hard, but I did it. So, when my mom's mom died, I felt obligated to be there for her as well, so I flew off to Illinois to do that funeral also. However, on the flight back home I was confronted with an entirely new thought.

Chapter Sixteen

I was flying non-stop from Chicago, Illinois to Tokyo's Narita Airport when I had a strange epiphany somewhere over the Pacific Ocean. Being a Seventh-day Adventist, I had been taught the importance of keeping the Ten Commandments, especially the fourth commandment which told us to keep the Sabbath holy. Now, as everyone knows, the Sabbath was Saturday, so I was taught that from Sundown Friday to Sundown Saturday, the Sabbath was to be observed.

That was on my mind when I flew across the International Date Line because it suddenly became apparent that it would have been possible to leave one side of the planet and get to the other side and completely skip the Sabbath. That segued to another thought, "What would I do if I was living in a place that had 24 hours of darkness or light?" The Sabbath was so important that I knew I needed to figure this out.

When I got back to our mission base, I called up the Far Eastern Division of Adventists, as that was the larger region at the time, and talked to the vice-president. I asked him what we would do if we encountered 24 hours of darkness or light? He said that the answer was rather simple. They simply set the Sabbath from 6pm to 6pm.

His answer rocked my world because in Adventist theology it was said that the Roman Catholic church had changed the "times" and moved the Sabbath from Saturday to Sunday so that in essence, they had become the Anti-Christ. I had preached to others about how the Catholic church had deceived all the Evangelical church world and it was the key cog to everything prophetic in my mind. Now, the Adventist officials were telling me that we, the Adventists, had also changed the times of the Sabbath when it was convenient for us to do so.

That realization was like an earthquake and my Adventist faith shattered. I know it does not sound like much at the time but because I had never questioned my doctrine and simply took what I had been taught at face value but the mere idea that we could change times as well threw me off. I felt as though I could justify this position but then the Catholic Church and most Evangelicals thought that they could justify going to church on Sunday as well. What did that mean?

I was not equipped to question my church or my faith and when the anger that I was already feeling rose up and wrapped its tentacles around my faith I was no match for the rage, insanity and emotional reactivity that flew forth. I instantly felt deceived. I mean, how could a denomination tell someone such a blatant lie? I did not know what to do so I started studying religion, the Bible, and the different church denominations all from an intellectual point of view.

There was no internet at the time, so I had to find books that described the different denominations and determined to read by Bible through from Genesis to Revelation with a notebook. I was going to try to figure out what the Bible taught instead of what I had been taught.

Have you ever wondered what the Bible actually said in terms of how we should live? There are some groups that say you have to get baptized by being dunked in water, others said you could be sprinkled. Some groups said you should allow the Holy Spirit to be fully alive within you and then you could heal and cast out demons while others said that those powers ceased when the Apostles died. There are so many different types of beliefs. Some say women can lead and others say, "no, no."

I wanted to know what was the truth and it was the best thing I ever did. The Bible does tell us that when Jesus was walking on this planet that He told His disciples that it would be better for them if He went away as the Holy Spirit would then lead, guide, and direct them. All of us, once we accept Jesus as our Savior, are filled with the Holy Spirit so what is possible?

All I know is that the Bible is a wonderful way to understand Jesus so I would recommend to each of you that you check it out for yourselves.

My journey led me away from the Seventh-day Adventist movement but even though I tried to move on it was hard because the legalistic message of having to appease God was pushed down deep inside of me.

Chapter Seventeen

A new world opened for me upon my return from Japan. I had no idea as to where I fit. Leaving the Adventist church meant leaving friends and relationships and I had no idea what to do. People looked at me as though we had gone to hell and others would no longer want to be around me because they felt as though I would lead them astray.

It is a funny thing about religion. It is the foundation for many but when it gets rocked and that foundation crumbles it is hard to hold on to any aspect of God. The denomination tried to help me out by providing some assistance relocating but by feelings of being betrayed were too much and once again the great foundation of lies that I was raised in rose up and I started seeing everyone through a lens of paranoia.

My legacy of being lied to and feeling betrayed stirred many things within me and so I tried the best I could to grasp at anything that would make sense. When I came back from Japan I landed in Los Angeles and spent a few weeks out near San Bernadino and thought that perhaps I would get a master's degree in health care administration and work in a hospital or nursing home. I could help people and would not have to teach or guide people in their theology, as mine was pretty messy and confusing at that point in time.

I started attending a Missionary Baptist Church which eventually led me to a Church of Christ. I picked Church of Christ because I had been reading some books from Max Lucado which really taught a lot about God's grace and Max was a Church of Christ pastor. I went to the church excited but learned early on that the Church of Christ was similar to the Adventist Church with a lot of legalism thrown into the mix. They taught that you could not have any musical instruments in the church as the Bible forbid it.

That was a new teaching for me and so everyone sang hymns acapella which was great if you could carry a tune. I was tune challenged and it was a struggle. Plus, the church allowed a piano to be in the multi-purpose room, not in the sanctuary of the church.

I did not last long in that movement but did manage to find my way to the Independent Christian Churches where I found a good balance for me at that time. Part of my journey

If you are finding a less than stellar path there is a possibility that the trauma of those early days is still leading you even though you may be doing everything you can to avoid it.

There is this unique part of the brain called The Reticular Activating System, or the RAS, that is found in your brain stem. It is the size of a pencil and only two inches long. That system is like the algorithm of the brain. It is the connection point between the conscious and unconscious part of the brain, and it is constantly analyzing our behavior to figure out what we will be focusing in on. You can see how it works if you have been one of those people who take the same route to work every day.

Eventually, the RAS figures out the path and knows that if you are heading in a certain direction where you are going. So much so that if you do not pay attention before you realize it you simply arrive at work with no real recollection of how you got there. The RAS kicked in and just directed you. Another example is when shopping for a new vehicle. Let us say that you want to buy a new truck. You get online and check out trucks and you stop at the New Nissan Titan. It looks cool and so you do some more research and are determined to check it out. Now, up to that point you have not seen a lot of them, but you are curious.

Your RAS will register that this is important to you and as you start to drive around all of a sudden you will start to see more and more of them. It is because the RAS has reset the algorithm and now you are looking for them subconsciously.

When we tell ourselves that we want to become like someone or when we tell ourselves that we do not want to be like someone, the someone is still the focus and inadvertently our RAS directs us to that behavior and it drives us, whether we are aware of it or not.

My life was one of reacting to my father. I did not want to be like him, and it consumed me. I wanted to be better, to overcome my past but inadvertently, what I was doing was setting my RAS to focus on my father.

As a result, I kept setting myself up and time after time I would find myself in situations that did not make any sense because I did not develop any awareness of what was actually happening. My survival skills were flawed so my actions were flawed. Thus, the power of emotional healing.

When I enrolled at Indiana State University after my return from Japan, I was determined to be a psychologist and help others with their problems but at the same time my own problems were so deep that I could barely breathe from the stench. Even though I realized that my past was terrible no matter how hard I tried I kept seeming to repeat aspects of it. I found myself thinking, "how was this possible?" "Was I cursed?" "Did God hate me?"

The frustration of the haunting behavior was tough to deal with, but I was determined to overcome it. I just had no idea where to go or what to do. I was hoping that by learning more about the mind it would set me free so even though I continued to seek out counseling, my story would either shock my therapist so that they got caught up in the story or they broke down in tears and were no longer of any use.

It was only the grace of God that kept me alive during this time. I started drinking again to hide the pain and tried to do anything, constructive or destructive, that would deaden the agony. I was miserable, lost more weight, and was losing my mind, sanity, and soul as well. This state of chaos continued for several months until a colleague at ISU invited me to attend church with her at the Maplewood Christian Church. I was shocked that anyone would invite me to a first day church (one that met on Sunday) but I knew I was desperate and so I went figuring that the Anti-Christ would grab me upon entering the evil church.

What I found amazed me because the people at that church accepted me as I was. I showed up expecting to find the ceiling collapsing but left with a wonderful sense of God's presence in my life. I made an appointment to speak to the pastor, Stan Eastman and he shared with me the simple message of God's grace, which somehow, I had repeatedly missed.

I felt that I needed to attend the Maplewood Christian Church, so I did. I went to adult Bible studies; I attended Sunday morning and evening services and I tried to learn all I could about God's love. It was a wonderful experience that culminated one Easter morning.

I was driving down highway 31 in Northern Indiana heading back to school when the Lord clearly told me that I needed to choose who I was going to serve. I instantly knew what that meant and with tears flowing agreed to really follow Jesus from my heart. I had finally come to the point where I knew that I could no longer do what I was doing without exploding and so as I cried,

I talked to Jesus, and for the first time in my life I was open and honest with Him and could hear Him breathe as He wrapped His arms around me.

Now this did not mean that I was healed but it did open up a dialogue with God and I started seeing God as a loving Father instead of Thor tossing down lightning bolts to get me.

It was three months after that day that a small Christian church in Atwood, Illinois called me to serve as their pastor and I became a first day pastor of a small flock who had no hope. Their building had burned down, and they had dwindled down to 29 souls who were trying to figure out if they had any purpose or not. I agreed to come and within one year an amazing thing occurred. We built a new building, the attendance shot up to 99, and the community was all abuzz.

At the time I had two kids, a small landscaping company and a small growing church and from all outward appearance's life was grand. I had a new lease on life and was chipping away at my doctoral degree in psychology, but one major problem remained. I had not allowed God to do any work on my soul. I was making outward choices that needed to be made but inwardly I was as rotten as before.

I just did not want to take God all that seriously. As a matter of fact, a minister friend and I went to see a movie when it came out. A movie that I am not proud to admit to seeing. It was an NC-17 rated movie called "Showgirls" and it was pretty much a pornographic movie. I felt as though it would not bother me to see it and my ministerial colleague also felt as though it was ok to see such a movie. At that point in my life, I was back to the perfect hypocrite. I served God publicly but inwardly I lived as I wanted. I still would only go so far when it came to God.

God, however, did not give up on me and started pestering me through the Holy Spirit. I was aggravated but could sense that God was calling me to take him seriously. I just did not want to do it but thought that perhaps I should try. Perhaps, perhaps, if I really put my all into getting to know Jesus, it would make me a better person.

I remembered back in college that there was this pastor in Kalamazoo that would get up and spend an hour with God every morning. He said it was the key and that we should all do it and I thought he was pretty much off his rocker. Who in their right mind would get up early to read their Bible and pray?

As I pondered what the Holy Spirit was telling me I decided that I would give it a try. I would get up early, grab my cup of coffee and my Bible and spend an hour with God every morning. I figured, "How hard could it be?"

Ha, it was terrible. The first morning I set out my Bible, had my hot java, closed my eyes, and prayed. I then read a bit from my Bible and looked at the clock and only five minutes had passed. I had determined to spend an hour with God, and I had never gone past 5 minutes. I took a deep breath and that first day I prayed for one minute and read my Bible for 59 minutes. One hour!

I adjusted it a bit from that point onward. I got into the routine of writing a letter to God in a prayer journal, putting down a list of names to pray for, and then I would read at least five chapters from the Bible, a habit that I still do years later. It has become one of the most important things that I do but at the time it seemed almost impossible.

Eventually, after about a year, I started looking forward to my hour in the morning and as I started to learn more about Jesus through this time a subtle change started to occur in my life. I found myself starting to really think there was more out there. I started to get the sense that God was greater than I had imagined but it was really hard to see it or experience it.

Chapter Eighteen

I tell people that I was going around as if I was a donut with no filling. There was this ache for something more, but my theological brain could only stretch so far. I thought that God was an active God in the past but outside of a moment here and there, it did not seem as though God was all that real today.

It was about this time that a middle-aged lady in my church, Janice, developed an issue with her leg. An infection set in, and the doctors said it was so bad that it was going to have to be removed. She told everyone at church, and I scheduled an appointment to stop by the day before she was to go into the hospital to pray with her. I did that for everyone who was going to have surgery because as a minister I knew it made them feel better. I should add that I never thought my prayers did much.

The day I was to go with her I had a lunch meeting in the town of Jasper, which was about 30 minutes south. I was meeting the owner of a music store and another area pastor there and we were going to have lunch and try to plan a rally or something for the next year. We arrived and I could tell the other minister was one of those guys who said "Praise the Lord" every other sentence. It was a bit annoying, but I hung out and then as we were leaving the place the music store owner told us something that happened in his life which was pretty cool. I said, "wow, that was great," but the older minister stopped and turned right to me and said, "You should say, "Praise the Lord."

I thought whatever and got in my car and started driving north. I got about halfway to my church when out of the blue I felt the most incredible sadness that I had ever experienced. It was followed by tears and then I started crying so hard that I had to pull off the side of the road. I could not stop crying and I felt so hollow. I knew that there had to be something more, so I told God that if this was how it was going to be I was going to walk away from ministry and from believing in Him.

After about 15 minutes I stopped crying and continued on my trek to Janice's house where she was waiting for prayer. I arrived and there was an older lady in her little apartment, and I told them that I was there to pray. The older lady said she would head home, she only lived a few apartments over, and I sat down across from Janice. She had an Afghan over her legs, but she showed me her leg and it looked terrible.

I comforted her and then I looked right at her and asked my question, "Janice, do you think God can heal your leg?" There was a pause and then she confidently said, "yes." At that moment I got chills all over my body and did not know what to do. I did not think God could heal her leg, but I was not about to tell her. Instead, I told her, "Ok, Janice, I am going to pray for me, then you pray for you and then I am going to pray that God would heal your leg."

She agreed so we bowed our heads and began. After I prayed for God to heal her leg, I opened my eyes and looked at her and she said her leg felt funny. I thought, right. It is your imagination. But when she pulled the blanket back, right before our eyes, her leg changed color and healed. I was so shocked that I told her to wait right there and ran down to the older lady's apartment and told her she had to come back.

When she got there, she took one look at Janice's leg and started praising the Lord. I was freaking out as this type of thing was not supposed to happen. It was then that Janice looked right at me and said, "This was for you, wasn't it?" I told her I had to go and promptly left.

I drove as fast as I could to my office and then got into the face of God. "What are you trying to do?" "I thought we had a deal, I left you alone and you and Satan left me alone?"

The next few months found many strange things happening. A church would call me up down the road and say that God had put it on their heart to ask me to come preach. I would be at a prayer meeting where everyone was getting prayed for and a lady would come to me and then say, "God told me not to pray for you." But then, in the Winter of 1996 I walked to the side door of the Loogootee Christian Church in Indiana, which was next door to the church parsonage, carrying my three-year-old daughter and when I got to the church doors they were unlocked, and the lights were on. I peered in and just assumed some of the worship team was at the church preparing for the weekends service but when I walked around the corner I was greeted by a man and a woman seated in the front pew.

I glanced around and there did not seem to be anyone else in the building so I politely asked them if I could help them. They informed me that they were looking for the pastor and so I told them I was the pastor and that I would be happy to talk with them. I also told them that I needed to run my daughter back home and then I would be right back.

After depositing my daughter back at my house, I called a friend of mine to come over to the church, just in case I needed reinforcements and went back in to see our guests. I sat directly across from them in the communion chairs that we had facing the congregation and asked them what I could do to assist.

They glanced at each other and then the lady said, "should we tell him?" I had no idea what they were about to say but judging by their appearance I was prepared for the worst. They were both dressed all in black with black hair. Their faces were white, and the man had a sword strapped to his side and they wore shirts that declared their allegiance to Satan.

The lady turned to me and said, "we are witches." Instantly the hair stood up on the back of my neck and I wanted to say, "thanks for coming see ya later." I refrained from doing so however and prayed silently for the strength that I needed to understand what was going on. I proceeded to ask them what brought them to the church, and they told me that they were tired of the voices that were going on in their heads and they wanted out. They were walking by the church and sensed God's presence there and knew that they could get help. They tried the door, and it was open, so they came in and sat down.

I talked with them, ended up baptizing the young man on the spot and eventually my friend, Keevin and I went to the man's home, which was decorated with upside down stolen crosses and helped him clean up the area and dedicate it to God. At one point we were taken into the man's bedroom, and he opened the lid on this cooler on the floor and a white gas like substance started coming out. It looked like fog.

I was officially freaked out and felt like I was in a horror movie. I prayed as fast as I could that God would protect us. I reached down and picked up the young man's evil robe and we spread it out on the floor, and I started putting things on it that needed to be discarded. We had books of chants and spells and other evil things as well. When we left the house, Keevin and I took the stuff and went out to my car and opened the trunk but before I put the stuff in there Keevin and I prayed that God would protect the trunk and us from the evil that we had just experienced.

We placed the robe and all the other stuff inside of my trunk and drove over to the church where we had a large burn barrel outside the back, near to my garage. We drove up and got out of the car and then Keevin and I looked at each other and were stumped. We really did not know what to do but after a brief discussion decided to burn the stuff that we had gotten from the guy's house.

We put it all inside the burn barrel and then I went into my garage and got out my container of gasoline and poured some on the stuff so that it would burn up faster. I wanted to make sure that all of it burned as I was officially creeped out.

Keevin and I lit a match, stood back from the barrel, and tossed the burning match into the barrel content on the knowledge that when the flames got wind of the gas fumes the contents of the barrel would go, "boom." But what actually happened was far different. The match did land on the stuff we were hoping to burn but even though the flame was burning the contents did not catch fire.

I turned to Keevin, and we started to pray. More matches were tossed in and eventually the contents, even though they were now soaked with gasoline, slowly started to burn. As they did a large cloud of smoke started to rise above the barrel and it rose into the air for about 20 feet and then, right before our eyes, it seemed to stop rising. It was as if there was a glass ceiling and the smoke started to build up at that point and then it started to swirl around a bit and then it started coming back down on the sides directly for Keevin and myself.

I was so scared that I could not even move. Keevin just reached up his hand and made the sign of the cross in the air and rebuked the smoke in the name of Jesus and it simply vanished into the air, it was gone.

We stood out there as the smoke tried one more time to intimidate us later and then eventually the contents of the barrel burned up and Keevin and I departed to our own homes without saying anything more to each other.

When I got back into my house it was early in the morning and I was terrified. I had no idea what we were dealing with and the idea that Satan was alive and well, that evil demons existed, was something that I did not want to face.

The next day I tried to forget what had happened the previous night and that worked until it got dark out. Once darkness came, it felt as though an evil presence enveloped the area all around our house. I had to walk from my house to the church and as I stepped outside chills covered my body and I stepped back into the house and shut the door. I was terrified to go outside. I really felt that Satan or something evil was standing in between the house and the church door and I could sense it, feel it, and was deathly afraid of it.

I had never met anyone who had told me of anything even close to what I had just experienced. In my mind I had hoped that Satan was not real, and that evil did not really exist. I was hoping for living a good life sort of thing because that was all that was really needed. That thought was blown out of the water the previous night and as I sat in my house afraid to go next door the name of a man came into my mind who I had heard speak in Terre Haute, Indiana years earlier.

His name was Ben Alexander, and he was a former spiritualist who led séances in England years earlier. He had formed a ministry called, "ESP" and I had heard him speak at the Maplewood Christian Church where he had shared the reality of Satan and how evil impacts our world. When I had heard him speak, I had thought he was a bit off but the night of fear, as I remember it, recalled his stories to my mind and I went to my library where I had placed a copy of his book. Even though I had never read the book it did have his contact information in it.

Ben lived outside of Tampa, Florida so I called information. Got his telephone number and called him up and remarkably, he answered. I was never so happy to talk with someone in my life and I quickly told him what had taken place and about my fear. He listened very patiently and then walked me through what to do. He shared with me the reality that God was more powerful than Satan. He reminded me of two Bible verses:

2 Timothy 1:7, "for God gave us a spirit not of fear but of power and love and self-control."

1 John 4:4, "for He who is in you is greater than he who is in the world."

Ben reminded me that God was in me, and that God was more powerful than evil. He encouraged me and told me that I had nothing to be afraid of. He told me to claim the power of God and to walk outside and be confident. I talked with him for a while longer and then hung up the phone and prayed like I had never prayed before.

I then walked to my door, opened it up and started reciting those two verses aloud as I slowly walked from my house to the church. I was afraid and I knew that Satan wanted me to fear him, but it was a battle, and I knew with all of my heart that God was greater. I made it to the church and in my spirit, I knew God was telling me that I was not to be afraid.

Of course, I thought my class in spiritual warfare was over, but God was not done working yet. A few years earlier I had met a pastor from a Pentecostal church at the Promise Keepers Clergy Conference in Atlanta, Georgia. During that conference we were challenged to find someone who had a different belief system that we had and to ask them to pray for us. I had always spoken ill of the Pentecostals, so I felt as though I needed to ask a Pentecostal to pray for me. When I got this idea, I had no idea how to find one but as I looked around, I noticed the guy in front of me so I tapped him on his shoulder and asked, "You wouldn't have to be a Pentecostal pastor would you?"

Remarkably, he was a Church of God, Cleveland, Tennessee pastor. That denomination was Pentecostal, and I told him that I felt he needed to pray for me. While he prayed for me, I prayed for God to protect me, but all went well, and we traded business cards and that was that. I immediately forgot all about it. Until a few years later when he called me out of the blue.

It was after my two experiences that he called me up one evening and said, "do you remember me?" I vaguely remembered him and then he told me something that blew me away. He said he had been praying and God had told him to call me up and invite me to come to his church, in Northern Ohio to preach. I said, "Excuse me, God said what?" He told me that he was sure I was to come to his church to preach. I thought he was crazy but with all that had been happening in my life I was afraid to rule anything out. I told him I would pray about it and so I did, and it was strange, but I did sense, in some deep, inner way, that I was to go to Ohio to preach.

It did not make any sense, but my family and I packed up and made the drive through an ice storm, in the end of January, during Super Bowl Sunday for Pete's sake. We showed up in Ohio and he welcomed us into his home. He did not know us from Adam but treated us like long lost kin folk. It was weird and he showed us around his little church and told us that his church had two services and that I was to preach at each one and then preach again on Sunday night.

I had prepared a sermon and knew that I could wing one for Sunday night, so I was not too worried about it. I was a little nervous about being in a Pentecostal church as I had never ever stepped foot in one in my entire life because to be honest with you, I thought that the spirit in the Pentecostal church was something that was not from God.

We ventured off to the church, New Life Church of God, and I got there early to greet everyone who was coming to church. It was a small building that could probably hold 120 people if everyone packed in tight. The service started and Dode leaned over to me and said, "just preach whatever God has put on your heart and then ask if anyone wants to be prayed for at the end." It made sense so when it came time to preach, I got up, walked over to the pulpit and as I spread out my notes to begin my sermon it was as if God shut off my brain.

I did not know what to say and I paused as I looked out over the people and they all went, "ooooooh." I felt like it was my first sermon and then words started coming to my mind and I just started talking. It was the most powerful sermon I had ever preached, and it went on for about 2 hours. People went home, got other people, and then brought them back to church while I was speaking. It was crazy and unlike anything else I had ever been a part of or seen.

Then, when I asked if anyone wanted prayer, the entire church formed a line, and they started coming up. I prayed for whatever they asked for and it was a wonderful time, and it was a draining time. Finally, I was down to one last lady and as she came closer to the front she started weeping uncontrollably. I felt empathy for her. She was in her late 20's, I think, and was accompanied but what I took to be her mother. The poor lady was in misery and as she got closer, she almost collapsed from the sobs. I had her sit in the front pew and then told her I was going to pray for her.

When I approached her, she started wailing all the more and so I stepped back and asked her mother, who later I discovered was her friend, what had happened to the lady. She told me that the lady had been sexually molested and was battling with recovering from that. I instantly thought I understood. She had come up for prayer, I was a male stranger, and so I figured my presence had unsettled her.

I cautiously approached her again and stepped to the side so I would not be directly in front of her and calmly shared with her that I was going to pray for her. She nodded her understanding and then I went to lay my hand on her head and right before I touched her, she went berserk. She started slamming her head into the corner of the wooden pew and would not stop. I thought she was going to kill herself, so I instructed the women nearby to lay her on the floor as I thought perhaps, she was having a seizure.

However, when they laid her on the floor, she kept lifting up her head and moaning loudly and then slamming her head on the hard wooden floor. I did not know what to do so I sat down on the floor by her head and cradled her head in my hands to try to prevent her from hurting herself.

It all happened so fast that I was operating on sheer reflex but then as I held her head, she tipped her head back and looked right into my eyes and a deep masculine voice came out of her that said, "She's ours."

Now, I had only seen one horror movie in my life and that was the movie, "Poltergeist," and I was scared so much in that movie that I swore off all evil type movies. Well, suddenly I was living a horror movie and after the woman screamed and that deep voice talked to me, I knew in an instant that I was in for a battle with a demon. I prayed like never before and all the people in the church prayed. I really do not know how long it took, but eventually the woman vomited, well it looked like she did, but nothing came out and then she fell asleep and woke up calm and no idea what had just happened.

She got up off the floor and was praising Jesus and everyone was so excited and yet I felt like a wet noodle on the floor. What had just happened? I was told by the pastor that I had just cast out a demon. I could not comprehend that especially because I did not believe that demons could actually possess a person.

Eventually, everyone left the church and a big group of us went to Pizza Hut where I could not eat as I still was spinning from what was happening.

After months of these intense, almost crazy experiences, I developed gastritis and was a nervous wreck. It was not because of the experiences that I developed the gastritis it was because I now knew that God was real, that spiritual warfare was real, that Satan was real, and that God was now wanting me to get serious about my faith and serving Him. I knew that meant giving up many of my small sins, allowing Him total access to my heart and that scared me more than anything else. It meant that I had to be vulnerable, to trust God like never before.

From that time onward I knew, there would never be any turning back because there was no doubt about the fact that Satan was real, and he was out to destroy.

When I was in Loogootee, I discovered who Jesus was and it transformed me, or should say that it finally set me on the right path so God could transform me into His character and image as I fell deeper and deeper in love with Him. I finally started to understand what loving God was all about and the seeds finally started to grow and my faith went from worrying about leaving God to understanding and knowing that I would never walk away from the living and all powerful God, even if at times, I did not understand Him or struggled with trusting Him.

Yet, I want to be clear here. Just because I had these amazing experiences did not mean that I knew how to live. I was damaged by the past and was trying to put it all together, but I still did not trust anyone and had no one in my life who was telling me how I should balance it all. I needed a mentor, a godly person, someone who could speak truth into my life. But alas, there was an incredible void. I tried to keep all the trauma pushed down deep inside of me and what my brain wanted to do and what my emotions often told me to do were very far apart.

Chapter Nineteen

My adventures in the Independent Christian Churches continued and in January of 2000, I accepted a call to become the Senior Pastor of the Central Christian Church in Snohomish, Washington. Western Washington was this gem of a place. It was luscious, green, full of beauty, but it rained or at least misted most days. There was a sort of cloud covered environment and different days were brighter, but you really did not see the sun a lot. It drove many people bonkers, but I found the overall beauty of the place intoxicating.

Western Washington was classified by church growth experts as a more difficult area to plant a church as there were many people who did not believe in God. It was an overall accepting place that instead of believing in one God, really believed in whatever version of God you wanted to design. With all the natural beauty there were many who believed that God was more like mother nature, and you had to be one with the environment. It provided quite a challenge and so I moved to Washington, was able to buy my first house and went to work at the church.

I arrived when the church had been averaging about 166 in worship and within one year the attendance skyrocketed to 400 and I was inundated with new believers and forced to figure out how to deal with them. Now in all my training to be a minister no one actually showed me anything about doing the work of ministry. I could preach a good sermon, parse Greek and Hebrew, study the Bible in the original languages but to work with the people in the church. To help people deal with conflict? That was sort of like a lab that never ended. Learning on the go which meant some things I did well and some things I did not do well.

I had become one of those guys who went to problem churches and helped them turn around. I would spend a couple of years at each place and then the church would grow, and I would leave and head off to another church. Each church I went to was full of infighting, conflict and the membership was declining. I would come in and primarily by using my personality, get everyone excited and the church would grow. Yeah!

Inevitably, some in the church would not like the fact that the church was growing rapidly and so there was always conflict. It was usually over the strangest things. The use of a piano or organ; the type of music one sang; the hours one would work; the primary role of the pastor—-evangelist to reach the lost or chaplain to take care of the saved? I was once at a church where we changed the brand of donuts from Krispy Kreme to Publix to save cost and it was as if a world war had been started. People were incensed, there was even talk of firing the senior pastor. Over donuts!

God's imperfect people can mean well but sometimes they do not do the right thing. I call these individuals "well intentioned dragons." They mean well but leave scarred earth wherever they go.

My years of trying to be a pastor was starting to take its toll on me. Going to negative church to negative church started to create some further mistrust and I started seeing church people as more negative than positive. This in turn led to a line of thinking that I knew what was best and so I had to convince the church leaders to follow me. Being an addict in recovery that manipulation part of me was never far behind and what I did not realize at the time was my type of leadership was passion driven with a sprinkle of manipulation and probably a lot of passive aggressiveness.

The church where I was serving in Snohomish started having difficulty with the former senior pastor, whose family stayed in the church leadership, and a power encounter broke out that almost broke me. After fighting it for almost a year I just resigned and for a period of one month prayed about what I should do next.

At that time, I had also founded a Christian Counseling center (family4today.org) as I had become a licensed professional counselor in the State of Washington and was imploring the Lord if that is where He wanted me to serve during this next season of my life. However, God had another plan. I prayed for 30 days that God would make it clear what my next step would be. I placed my life squarely in His hands and during that time I turned down a Christian Church in Kansas City, Missouri and one near Columbus, Ohio as they just did not set right with my spirit.

Finally, it became apparent that I was to plant a church and an area in Western Washington popped into my mind. It was called Sultan and a Real Estate friend of mine referred to Sultan as the "armpit of the world." It was a town of about 4,000 people that was a backwater, highly political quagmire of a town that really needed a contemporary church. Somehow, I had a burden for that community and ended up getting with 8 adults in an attempt to plant a new church. We called it Cornerstone...a church for the community.

It was going to be a church that accepted people where they were and partnered with them on a journey of hope, healing, and renewal. I thought and prayed long and hard about what type of church to plant and for some reason I felt as though we should reach out to the burned, bored, and bypassed. We would be the killer "b" church, lol.

We started meeting in a small gathering and praying hard for a miracle. I had told God that I needed $100,000 for the first year to make sure everything worked out, but we were only able to raise about $5,000 starting out. I had to work part time at another church and also work as much as I could at my counseling center, but I wanted to devote everything I had to the church.

We started meeting in January and by the time Easter rolled around we were ready to move to the high school and do a mailing to announce that a new church was here. We had grown to about 30 people at the time, had rented an office in Sultan and had made an agreement to rent the high school commons weekly to hold worship services.

We sent out our mailer and low and behold when Easter rolled around, we had close to 130 people gather in the commons to help celebrate the resurrection of Jesus Christ. It felt great and we never looked back. We grew, all sorts of disenfranchised people came, and the dynamics of the church felt really good. But there is this thing that comes with damaged people? Trauma, conflict, pain, and we had to deal with it all.

I thought being in a church where people could be honest and up front about what they were going through would be a good thing. Finally, no more hypocrisy or at least less of it. I wanted everyone, from the leaders on down, to be authentic and talk about life in a real way which also included our struggles and our victories.

It confirmed my thought that people just needed to be pointed to Jesus and He would do the rest. My philosophy had been based on two key books. *Messy Spirituality* by Michael Yaconelli and *What's So Amazing About Grace* by Philip Yancey.

Yaconelli had challenged me to really make sure that I was not the gate keeper for who could come to Christ. Of course, he did not use that terminology but instead called such people "Kingdom Monitors."

In his book, "Messy Spirituality," he stated on page 47:

> Nothing makes people in the church angrier than grace. It is ironic: we stumble into a party we were not invited to and find the uninvited standing at the door making sure no other uninvited get in. Then a strange phenomenon occurs: as soon as we are included in the party because of Jesus' irresponsible love, we decide to make grace "more responsible" by becoming self-appointed Kingdom Monitors, guarding the kingdom of God, keeping the riffraff out (which, as I understand it, are who the kingdom of God is supposed to include.)

I did not want to be a Kingdom Monitor. I wanted the Holy Spirit to be the Kingdom Monitor and the only thing I wanted to do was to shout to the people that Jesus loves them. It sounded so wonderful to have a church where the people could really understand the love of God. I mean what could be wrong with that?

Another quote that impacted me was from Yancey, where he shared a story about a friend of his who works with the down and out in Chicago, on page 11:

> A prostitute came to me in wretched straits, homeless, sick, unable to buy food for her two year old daughter. Through sobs and tears, she told me she had been renting out her daughter—two years old! —to men interested in kinky sex. She made more renting out her daughter for an hour than she could earn on her own in a night. She had to do it, she said, to support her own drug habit. I could hardly bear hearing her sordid story. For one thing, it made me legally liable—I am required to report cases of child abuse. I had no idea what to say to this woman.

> At last, I asked her if she had ever thought of going to a church for help. I will never forget the look of pure, naïve shock that crossed her face. "Church!" she cried. "Why would I ever go there? I was already feeling terrible about myself. They would just make me feel worse."

The church thrived as we opened up our hearts and minds. We were like a 911 hospital and there was constant activity. For a while I thought the church was actually going to find its footing and become a cultural changing life force but instead, all the people proved to be challenging on every level.

I still think it is a great idea to have an authentic church, but the church lasted for only four years and then slowly fell apart as people moved away, the economy changed, and I think because it was so intense. There were many amazing moments, we baptized over 100 people in the first year alone, but some did not want to change and so their dysfunction impacted everyone else. It was one thing to talk about our issues, but it was another to be in denial and not want to get better or to heal.

My therapy church experiment ended, and I moved on to another church where I took a small group and grew that church, or should I say, God grew that church to a large church of over 1,000. It was cool to be a pastor of a large church, but it was all about administration and that was one thing that was really challenging. I also started working more. I was doing more at the church and what I soon realized was that there was never time enough to get everything done.

When you pastor a large church everyone wants to speak with you, all the church conferences in the area want you to speak, smaller churches want to partner for resources and then there is just "more" people. Funerals, weddings, events, parties, celebrations, programs and such.

I tried balancing everything but it was proving to be difficult. Someone told me that people in the church needed Jesus more than people outside of the church and what I think they really meant to say was that people are damaged. They take time, love, patience and more time. As the church grew and became more successful there was less time to sleep, sermon preparation got cut and I seemed to go from crisis to crisis.

I thrived but my soul ached.

I knew I was reaching a precipice when I decided to launch a program at the church called the "Bowl Patrol." It involved getting people to come to the church and then we would divide up in teams and head out into the community and go door to door at the businesses and clean their toilets and bathrooms. We just wanted to be a gift.

I thought this was an amazing idea and when it came time to pull it off we had around ten people show up, from over a thousand and I became disillusioned. I had this depressing epiphany that people wanted to be ministered to but did not want to actually minister to others, unless it was convenient.

Now, I am not saying that epiphany was accurate. What I am saying is that my frustration level was used by God to water some seeds that had been dormant in me for quite some time.

I was the pastor of a large church, we had small groups, a killer worship team, an amazing reach, a cool coffee shop and we met in a converted old movie theater. What could be cooler than that?

Well, you can guess what happened. I burned out. The past of always trying to do everything for everyone just became too much and I crumbled under the load and the depression just permeated my spirit. I knew that I had to leave so I made the call to leave Washington and head back to the area of the country that I knew best, Florida.

I moved down to Sanford, Florida where I became the pastor of the Safeharbor Christian Church.

***As a reminder, remember that just because you got out of an abusive situation and that part of your life ended does not mean you know how to live. I cannot stress enough how the underlying issues are those that really need to be addressed. Clinical Trauma Counseling is a very important part of the healing process as is a good relationship with God. God allows us to see ourselves as "valuable," just because He made us that way. It is not because of what we do, how we look, or how much money we make. Our value is intrinsic, and it comes from God the moment we are conceived.

I had many lessons to learn in life after I got out of the great abuse. I had been molested, controlled, trafficked, beaten, ridiculed, bullied, to name just a few. I then took all of that and became a cocaine and sex addict, really, I tried to use anything I could to keep myself from feeling and dealing with reality.

I note this because it is important to realize that healing happens, but it is a process that never ends. Our goal is to stay on the healing path as we move forward.

Bob Carlisle, in his song, "We Fall Down," tells a story which I am going to paraphrase. He said there was this guy who walked to work every day. He was having a tough time in life but on his walk, he would go right in front of this monastery that had big walls and an iron gate. He could look in and see all the monks and they all seemed so happy, and he was not.

Day after day he found himself wondering what they were doing differently.

Then one day as he walked by there was a monk outside of the gate and he took the opportunity to speak with him. He asked the monk why he was so happy and contented looking. He asked what he could do to be more like the monk.

The monk straightened, looked into his eyes (dramatic effect) and then replied that it was easy. "When you fall down, get back up." Stunned the man walked away.

This is an important step from healing from trauma. You will fall down but growth is measured by how long you stay down when you fall. Do you wallow in it? Do you give up? Do you say why try anymore it impossible? Or do you get back up as quickly as you can, wipe yourself off, and keep on going.

One of the biggest keys of my growth is that fact that I am learning to get up faster and to stop dwelling on the negative. I check my thoughts. I recenter them on God. I remind myself that I have value. I tell myself I cannot do anything about the past. I emphasize in my cranium that just because I feel a certain way does not make it true.

The Bible says that the truth sets us free. I aim for that!

Chapter Twenty

When I came to Florida it was with grand plans. I was able to buy a nice house, settle in close to the church and I thought it was going to be great because as Disney says on their gates of their property, "it is the happiest place on earth." The church started small and then grew and as it grew, we had to go to two services, the church became more multi-cultural, and the church members started to feel uncomfortable.

I could see what was going on so I tried as best I could to be all things for each of them. I hired a youth minister, our worship was top notch, we had weekly study groups and yet it was never enough. (Sound familiar)

It was during my time at Safeharbor that I started to really get more involved in the motorcycle world. Earlier in my life I served at a church that was seven miles from the HQ of the Christian Motorcycle Association (CMA) in Hatfield, Arkansas and I would do many things with the members and leaders there. I was friends with the Chairman and those were good memories. I now decided to join the local chapter of CMA and started riding with them.

The freedom of the open road and the urgent call to share the love of Jesus with everyone was a passion of mine and so it became easy to do and soon more and more people started hanging around with me who shared a similar passion.

I had gotten my first motorcycle when I was just a little kid. We lived in Ortonville, Michigan at the time and my dad thought it would be a good idea for an eight-year-old to have his own Suzuki 50. My older brother and I got matching bikes and so we would ride them around the 80-acre farm that we owned, and it was a blast. My love of motorcycles grew, and I became fascinated with Evel Knievel and would sit in front of the television any time one of his jumps would be televised. I would secretly play like I was Evel with my yellow, banana seat Schwinn bike and you could find me jumping ramps all over the place.

I eventually ended up with a Honda 175 Enduro when we lived in Miami and I would ride that bike and jump off more sophisticated ramps made from dirt, yes, I was an idiot, but I never crashed but had many shots of adrenaline.

This led to my eventual purchase of a 125 motorcycle to ride on trails and then back in the early 2000's I decided to start riding a whole lot more and purchased a Yamaha and started commuting to my church on the bike. That bike grew until eventually I was on my black Harley Davidson Street Glide. I love the feel of the wind on my face and legs, and you can have the worst kind of day but if you are able to ride it seems as though the wind just blows it all away.

When I was a pastor in Snohomish, Washington I became friends with Pastor Dean Ekloff. Dean was the pastor the Midnight Cry Church, which was a biker church in Snohomish. He was a big, burly kind of guy and if you saw him, he was going to wrap you up in a big hug and greet you with a huge smile. He had been the town drunk in Snohomish when God got a hold of him and radically changed his life. Since that time, he went out and became a radical disciple of Jesus and was part of the Christian Crusader Motorcycle Ministry up in the Pacific Northwest.

Dean planted some amazing seeds in my heart because the church I planted in Sultan shared an openness with Midnight Cry.

Hanging around Dean showed me how important it was to be a daily evangelist and how important it was to stop judging people and start loving on them.

When I got to Florida and started riding all around it soon became clear that God was leading me on a path that I was unprepared for. I thought that I had been called to the "Gospel Ministry" and that there was only ONE way to be a pastor. It was from the pulpit and even though I kept trying to do that it just seemed as though I was digging a bigger and bigger hole.

I loved God and just found myself becoming frustrated with God's people. As a result, I started doing more and more away from the church and more and more on the motorcycle. It soon became apparent that I needed to transition for my own mental health.

I had started seeing a counselor for my own stability, had to get on Prozac because I was so stressed out. (Isn't that strange that I was never medicated when I was going through all of my trauma but then when I took away the drugs and stuff, I was a mess.)

I used my own counseling license and went to work at a counseling center and started attending motorcycle rallies. I still wore the CMA patch but that soon led to an independent Christian patch. I tried to encourage whoever came into my path and dropped all of my pretense and protective coat. I had finally learned that I could not do it all, that I was not Superman and that I was a damaged and imperfect dude who needed Jesus more each day.

I started to heal on every level. I started to laugh without the weight of the world. I started to see that I did not have to do everything for everyone and that I could actually be "me." I started rolling up my sleeves to show my tattoos instead of hiding them in shame and worry. In other words, I finally accepted that Jesus loved me just as I am, not as He wanted me to be.

I had heard the statement, "Jesus loves you just as you are, but he wants you to become more like Jesus." It implied to me that I had to become just like Jesus to truly fit into the heaven crowd. It was a crushing responsibility for a guy who grew up with no self-esteem in a legalistic church. I tried to be perfect but that only got me an ulcer. I finally realized that Jesus loves me just as I am because no one is as Jesus really wants them to be. It is His grace that covers me and as a result, God sees me as Jesus. Jesus, however, knows the truth. I am this imperfect dude who fails more than succeeds but who will never give up because I truly love Jesus.

My heart for ministry to the broken increased and my lifelong passion to help others really took over.

There is a passage in the Old Testament book of Ezekiel where God tells Ezekiel to prophecy to the Shepards (our equivalent of pastors) in Ezekiel 34:4. God tells those who profess to be godly shepherds:

> The weak you have not strengthened, the sick you have not healed, the injured you have not bound up, the strayed you have not brought back, the lost you have not sought, and with force and harshness you have ruled them. So, they were scattered, because there was no shepherd, and they became food for all the wild beasts.

It was a stunning rebuke and a reminder that as God's people we are all called with a strong mission. Isaiah 61:1-2 and Luke 4:18-19 create the call for each of us:

> The Spirit of the Lord is upon me, because he has anointed me to proclaim good news to the poor. He has sent me to proclaim liberty

to the captives and recovering of sight to the blind, to set at liberty those who are oppressed, to proclaim the year of the Lord's favor.

I had finally come to the point where I realized that I was a damaged individual who really needed to go out and reach damaged individuals like me. I had been trying to fit into a mold that was not designed for me and the more I tried to fit into the perfect role of church or be the person that "looked" like they had it all together, well, that just seemed to cause self-destruction.

I needed to embrace me, the work on my healing path, to allow God to do whatever it was that He wanted to do in my life, and most importantly...I had to reach out to others powered by His Holy Spirit within me.

My focus turned to motorcycle outreach, and I knew that I needed to be a motorcycle Chaplain to my community but more importantly, there was a group of hurting people that I would reach out to and assist. It meant coming full circle.

Chapter Twenty-One

Growing up I thought my life was normal. All the abuse, my dad being a felon, the early sexual molestation and trafficking, the ridicule and humiliation, and the type of punishment we received when we acted out. I thought every kid experienced the same thing, so it did not seem abnormal to be treated so poorly. If we sat at the dinner table and told a joke and my dad was not in the "mood," we would be punished. If we fidgeted in church, we would be punished. If someone asked us to do something and we did not do it right then, we would be whipped.

We also were constantly ridiculed for having dirty underwear, a broom stick would be stuck under our legs and into our crotch and everyone would laugh, we would have to have our pants pulled down when we were spanked. The concept that sex could ever be a good thing was not ever taught but the chemical reaction of when we had a sexual release, orgasm, now that was taught and experienced.

There is this strange phenomenon that develops in boys. Even if they are molested they can get an erection and even against your will you can have an orgasm and just the fact that you had the orgasm releases dopamine in the brain that rushes to our Nucleus Accumbens, or the pleasure center of our brain, and we feel good even though we also feel dirty. This confused state of mind creates a false sense of "we must have wanted this" or this is all "my fault."

Sexual trauma for boys or girls can be devastating because our higher order logic does not kick in until we are around the age of 13 so we try to piece things together in whatever manner we can, and it often leads to a confused brain on the issue of sexuality. When you experience that much dopamine from sexuality and are struggling to make sense of what it all means the brain can lead us on a journey that leads to very self-destructive activities or views of ourselves.

My sense of sexuality was that it was bad. Yet it felt good. I loved the dopamine which made everything feel better in that moment, but I hated what was happening to me. It did not take too long before masturbation was introduced into the story and now, I could release my own dopamine, which gave me pleasure but more importantly took away the pain. It is why sexual addiction is all too prevalent in our culture. Many guys have discovered dopamine from a sexual release and have conditioned our brain to such an extent that if we are lonely, angry, sad, depressed or experience any negative emotions at all there is a way out. Finding that sexual release. Sexual Addiction is real and one of the first people to address the reality of Sexual Addiction was Patrick Carnes in the 1980's. He wrote the best book on the subject, "Out of the Shadows."

Our culture today wants to normalize abnormal sexual activity. The separation of love from sex means that many are only open to sexual experiences, and it does not matter with who. The term "addict" applies, and most would be diagnosed with what is referred to as a Process Addiction vs a Substance Addiction. A Process Addiction is a behavior that we do to get dopamine. Some of the common Process Addictions are sex, gambling, eating, computer gaming, cell phones, etc...

When I was growing up many were being molested and sold for sex. Some of the girls I knew would tell me that they were making money by having sex, but I just thought that was a norm, an option for those who wanted that. I had no idea that people were being forced to have sex, even though I was one of those people.

Human Trafficking is the second fastest criminal activities in the world. As of this writing, 2024, it generates over 150 billion dollars (about $460 per person in the US) a year and sex trafficking is responsible for close to 99 billion. According to the United Nations, one in 113 people are in danger of being trafficked at any moment worldwide. In the back of this book there is a list of statistics and things you can do to fight human trafficking.

My sexual experiences were distorted and then when you add that my dad was a leader in the church and that most who abused me or used me for sex were males who were also very active in the church, this creates a distortion of faith and God, and you start to see yourself as damaged but then you assume that everyone was just as damaged. It creates a lifelong battle of identity and if you are not careful you can become so desperate that you try to change your identity because you get caught into thinking, "If I could just be that...all would be better."

Chapter Twenty-Two

I moved to Florida with high expectations of what being a minister would entail and as that eroded God flamed into passion my desire to reach those who did not know who Jesus was. The Apostle Paul in Romans 15:20 said it this way:

> And thus, I make it my ambition to preach the gospel, not where Christ has already been named, lest I build on someone else's foundation but as it is written, 'those who have never been told of him will see, and those who have never heard will understand.'

Paul's call to the Gospel was summarized in Acts 26:16-18 ESV:

> But rise and stand upon your feet, for I have appeared to you for this purpose, to appoint you as a servant and witness to the things in which you have seen me and to those in which I will appear to you, delivering you from your people and from the Gentiles to whom I am sending you. To open their eyes, so that they may turn from darkness to light and from the power of Satan to God, that they may receive forgiveness of sins and a place among those who are sanctified by faith in me.

When I walked away from Safeharbor it was not a negative but rather it was a confirmation of why God saved me. I was wired to reach the burned, bored, and bypassed. I wanted to tell people about Jesus, and I also wanted to help those in bondage break the chains that held them captive. My two-fold ministry was born after I came through the hell that was my life. First, to tell people about Jesus and Second, to help them get free and to find hope, healing, and renewal.

This quest led me to co-found Bikers Against Trafficking, Inc with Rainey, my wife and together we have had the humble honor of being a part of a group of people spread across the United States and Canada who seek to be the hands and feet of Jesus.

Bikers Against Trafficking that is not for the faint of heart. Rather, it is a motorcycle ministry that seeks to eradicate human sex trafficking, although you do not have to ride to be a part. As part of the mission, we provide places to live, clinical trauma counseling, mentorship, education and anything that is needed to promote a healthy and balanced life.

When I was in college and started on my quest for ministry, I had thought that my past was a negative. All the experiences I did not want anyone to know about as the shame connected to them crippled me. I thought I was "less than" and had to learn through the many tough seasons of life that my past did not define my future, but rather it equipped me to reach out with a love and passion that defies all common sense.

My life is far from complete. I strive to grow with God daily and part of that process is allowing Him to heal my wounds of the past.

This little book is almost over but I have a few more thoughts that I would like to share. One is a humble realization, and the other are the current statistics and some brief information about human trafficking.

Thank you for joining me on this journey and if you would like to reach out to me, please feel free to do so via Doc@bikersagainsttrafficking.org

Peace out!

Summary on the Christian Life

I turned 59 this year and I wish that I could report that my spiritual life has reached an all-time high. Instead, the truth is far less glamorous. I seem to struggle with everything that I had previously thought that I had overcome even though for the last 23 years I have gotten up early and spent about an hour a day in a daily devotional time with God.

I read my Bible through several times a year, move from translation to translation every couple of years to keep me sharp, have taken graduate classes in theology (I mean, hey, I even went so far as to get a doctoral degree in ministry), have tried fasting for long periods of time and writing in a daily prayer journal but even though I am "doing" what I think are all the right things my spiritual sensitivity scale seems to register remarkably low.

The result is a life of incredible frustration. I keep trying to figure out God's will for my life and as I press in to listen for that still small voice all I seem to hear is static. My desire to do what God would have me to do has often resulted in pulling out a pair of dice and rolling or even worse I find myself walking into a Chinese restaurant and waiting expectantly for the fortune cookie as if God was going to somehow send me a message that was creatively carved out 'just for me' and placed in the midst of sugar and flour. I cannot tell you how many times I have been disappointed with the "fortune" that was revealed in those cookies. I mean outside of learning what numbers I should be playing for this week's lottery game I have not really had that much luck.

So, what gives? What am I doing wrong? How come when a scantily dressed gal swaggers by I have to remind my eyes to look away? How come when an overwhelming day arrives, I find myself wanting to reach for a Xanax? What is the deal with having to take a daily Prozac pill to keep from being over-reactive? Why do I still lose my temper? How come I often have trouble sleeping? How come I sometimes get upset about my wife's actions? Why, when I pray, does it seem that I am being blocked by some kryptonite so that my prayers seem to be so ineffective? Finally, why do I find myself muttering the word that I was taught as a kid to never say, "Crap," when it comes to my meager attempt to live for God with all that I have?

In case you are wondering, I just tossed out the concept of this chapter to a psychiatrist friend of mine who happens to be a Christian and he uncomfortably shuffled and in his most loving manner suggested that when the book reaches the hands of the publisher that they might want to soften this up a bit.

Of course, I understood right away. I mean who wants to admit that the life we are living is sometimes crappy and unstable, ok, maybe more times than not it is crappy and unstable? It is a whole lot easier heading to the bookstore or internet and checking out those books that are major bestsellers stressing the power of positive thoughts, that you can do anything, or be anyone you want to be. I keep waiting for one of the books to give me the secret for living an overcoming life but outside of ripping open my shirt to reveal the giant Superman "S" for being spiritual man, I still find that I am about the same after reading the book, although I do feel somewhat better knowing that I have helped the author hopefully afford college tuition for their kids (I know, a bit too crass)

As a result of my spiritual journey, I thought it might be novel to simply share the truth (as I understand it). In a nutshell it would go something like this. Life is often hard, sometimes bad things happen that do not make sense, God is always in the mix, but I am not sure how, and eventually this life will pass away, and we will have a great shack in heaven. Actually, that was fairly negative. Perhaps if I tried again I would say that I firmly believe that God is with me and because of that...even though things don't always make sense...I will never give up and so I will persevere (because He has told me that He who is in me is greater than he who is not in 1 Jn 4:4 and so I know that I have incredible inner strength) and learn to treasure each moment as a gift. Doesn't that sound better?

It is my goal in this book to simply share a few thoughts about living the spiritual life. I am doing so not because I am perfect but rather because I believe that we have to stop hiding in the dark and face our truth as it is. At times I am embarrassed and ashamed of my past. I often wish that I could simply erase my brain in hopes that the yuck from my past would dissolve as well.

Yet it remains. I am who I am and at this point the scars I wear can either be used for God's glory or I will have to hide them in shame and guilt.

I was talking to a young lady a couple of weeks ago who has some scars of her own and I asked her, "What is the purpose of your scars?" The moment I asked her that question I knew that I had to finish this little book about my life, even though I have been reluctantly chipping away at it for the last 19 years or so. To be honest with you I am terrified of this little book because I do not want to be known as that guy with that past but yet I also have to come to understand that because I have such a past, I can relate to people in a different manner.

It is a gift but one that was born through much pain and sorrow.

It is my hope that by taking an honest and open look into what my journey has looked like that it might give you hope that no matter where you find yourself, God can redeem and use you. Our Lord and Savior specializes in taking those who are messed up, burned out, and bypassed and reclaiming them for His glory (I mean take a look at the prodigal son).

One of my favorite books was written by Michael Yaconelli and is entitled, "Messy Spirituality." Listen to his reminder about the people of the Bible.

Look at the Bible. Its pages overflow with messy people. The biblical writers did not edit out the flaws of its heroes. Like Noah, for example. Everyone thought he was crazy. He certainly was a little strange, but Noah was also courageous, a man of great faith and strong will. Against the backdrop of unrelenting ridicule, Noah built a huge ark in the middle of the desert because God told him it was going to rain. No one believed him, but the rains did come, and the flood happened, and after the water receded, Noah triumphantly left the boat, got drunk and got naked.

What? Drunk and naked? I do not recall any of my Bible teachers or pastors talking about Noah's.... uh...moment of indiscretion...er.... weakness...um...failure. The Noah I've always heard about was fiercely faithful, irrepressibly independent, and relentlessly resolute. Noah was the model of great faith. Very few ever refer to Noah's losing battle with wine. Maybe being strong and faithful has its downside. Maybe for flood survivors life is more complicated than we would like to think, and maybe even Noah could have bouts of depression and loneliness.

Why should I be surprised? Turns out all of the biblical characters were a complex mix or strengths and weaknesses. David, Abraham, Lot, Saul, Solomon, Rahab, and Sarah were God loving, courageous, brilliant, fearless, loyal, passionate, committed holy men and women who were also murderers, adulterers, and manic depressives. They were men and women who could be gentle, holy, defenders of the faith one minute, and insecure, mentally unstable, unbelieving, shrewd, lying, grudge-holding tyrants the next.

You might say Christianity has a tradition of messy spirituality. Messy prophets, messy kings, messy disciples, messy apostles.

When I read the words that Yaconelli wrote in his classic book I was immediately intrigued with his journey. He saw the Bible as a compilation of messy people trying to live out lives of faith and the reality was that most of them did not do so well. It gave me hope that I could be at least as good as some of those Bible folk. They reached up to the messy level. Perhaps, just perhaps, I could as well.

I also read another book entitled, "Scandalous Freedom" by Steve Brown and noticed a poem that was quite extraordinary. It was called, "Remember God Can Use Anybody!"

The next time you feel like GOD can't use you, just remember...

Noah was a drunk

Abraham was too old

Isaac was a daydreamer

Jacob was a liar

Leah was ugly

Joseph was abused

Moses had a stuttering problem

Gideon was afraid

Samson had long hair and was a womanizer

Rahab was a prostitute

Jeremiah and Timothy were too young

David had an affair and was a murderer

Elijah was suicidal

Isaiah preached naked

Jonah ran from God

Naomi was a widow

Job went bankrupt

Peter denied Christ

The Disciples fell asleep while praying

Martha worried about everything

Mary Magdalene was... well you know...

The Samaritan woman was divorced, more than once

Zaccheus was too small

Saul was too religious

Timothy had an ulcer...AND

Lazarus was dead!

I think it is important for us to remember that Bible is full of characters. Characters like you and characters like me. Average people who God shined the spotlight upon so that we could see how they overcame situations that often were overwhelming. In other words, the Bible gives hope to us all because it reveals a pathway of usefulness and grace. We are imperfect people who are simply trying to live for Jesus in a complicated world, and it is complicated. The questions of ethics, sexuality, church... Who knows the right answer.

Yet, through it all, God is good, God is love, God has the power, and we have hope.

We are nearing the close of this story. As it stands today, I am part of a non-profit motorcycle ministry, BikersAgainstTrafficking.org and I also run a small counseling ministry Family4Today.org and run an addiction treatment center, SojournersRecovery.org I also dabble in other small businesses as I am an addict and am always running around things in my little cranium.

My spiritual and healing journey continues and as I look back over my life, I see what God has turned to His glory. There is not a person that I have ever met that I cannot identify with in some manner. I hope that God can use my story so that everyone can have hope. I truly believe that if God could save me...he could save anyone! If God could use me, then he could also use anyone. Including YOU.

There is no, oops, God can no longer use you. It does not matter what your past entails. What matters is your future and if you turn that future over to God right now then He can do more than you could ever imagine. Never let anyone tell you that God cannot use you. The world in which we live is full of broken people and God can use them all. No matter what you did, no matter what was done to you. God has a plan for your life and you need to remember that God has perfected the "recall." He will never give up on you and perhaps you should not either.

So, get back up, wipe off the dirt and keep on keeping on.

A Few Thoughts on Suffering

When I became a Christian, I ordered the "Midas gold package." That meant that I wanted the promise that God had given to the Children of Israel in the Old Testament which said that no disease or ailment was supposed to afflict me. It also meant that God would take care of all my needs and that He would protect me by being a shield about me. I knew that because I lived in a Christian household only good things were supposed to happen. I was to have financial security and my family would never suffer any ill will and basically, I was to have the fairy tale, "and they all lived happily ever after ending." In other words, who would not want to be a Christian.

But then, life continued. And you know what? I think I got the wool pulled over my eyes. I say that because my Uncle Dan lived with us for most of his life and he was a quadriplegic. He hung out in the middle of our living room on a hospital bed and many nights he asked me to grab hold of his hands and ask God to heal them. I did and can remember straining in my attempts to coax God down from heaven so that my uncle could walk and move once again. I would open up my eyes in wild anticipation and nothing.

I can remember as a five-year-old being sexually abused. I recall being horse whipped as a form of discipline at the ripe old age of six. What was that all about? At the time I thought it was normal but as I got older, I kept looking back and questioning what transpired and as I did, I found myself asking, "Where did God go?" What happened to the shield around me thing when I was little? Later, divorce touched my life; my father ended up in prison; my family went on welfare and no matter how many times I claimed wealth...it never came. What did come was heartache, pain, despair, hopelessness.

A friend of mine was talking to me recently and was sharing about all the pain and agony going on in her life. At the end of her sharing, she looked up at me and said, "Life sucks." I was talking to another colleague who told me about their abusive past and then this guy said, "And I don't want to hear that God can use it for the good." (apparently that passage in Jeremiah 29:11 didn't really help him out). He got mad and almost ugly as he continued, "I just wish it wouldn't have happened." In other words, in his mind, it was not a worthy trade. The pain and suffering of the past was just plain bad. No one wants it, no one asks for it, and yet...all too often, many of us experience it.

What gives?

There are times when I really want to get into the face of God and allow my face to turn red as I scream out at him that it just is not fair. What was he thinking? Why did this have to happen? Why didn't he intervene? And my list could go on and on. I find myself wrestling with the words of the Biblical patriarch Job who went through a terrible ordeal...even though God said he was a righteous man.

Chuck Swindoll in his book, "Job" addressed the notion that many Christians have that God has a wonderful plan for His children: wonderful means—-comfortable, healthy, all bills paid, no debt, never sick, happily married with two well behaved children, a fulfilling, well-paying job, and the anticipation of nothing but blessing and success and prosperity forever. Unfortunately, [he adds] I think we may have misinterpreted a few things?

In the third chapter of the book of Job, the man for whom the book was titled was in a bad place. He had lost all comfort and was now dealing with lots of pain and a tremendous amount of hopelessness. But to really gain a proper perspective upon this man's life we need to quickly review what the first two chapters of the book of Job reveal about this man.

Job lived in a time when things were simpler. Technology as we know it simply did not exist (no ipads, iphones, cell phones, etc....) and a man's wealth was measured in animals. The more sheep and camels one had—the wealthier they were. Job lived in the area of the country that today, we define as the "Middle East," at a time that many scholars believe was when Moses was living in Midian.

Scholars believe that Moses became acquainted with Job during his time in Midian and as a result was inspired of God to write about this man's life. In setting the context of the biography of Job—-Moses gives us some important details about who the man was.

According to the first two chapters of the book of Job, Job was referred to as, "blameless, upright, a man who feared God and a man who turned away from evil." In other words, the writer of the book of Job wanted us to know without any skepticism or doubt that Job was a godly man who worshipped the Lord. He was not a rebellious sinner who doubted God, on the contrary...he was a man that lived for God.

The first two chapters of Job also tell us that Job was the greatest man of all the people of the East, a man of great wealth and influence who had been blessed with 7 sons, 3 daughters, and a lovely wife.

But then...into the life of this godly man comes tragedy on gigantic proportions. Within one day the stock market crashes and the Sabeans sweep in and steal all of his oxen and donkeys; the Chaldeans raid his camels and take them; fire from the sky comes down and burns up all his sheep and servants and to top it all off...a great wind comes sweeping across the valley and collapses the house of one of his children where all the kids were staying and crushing his ten kids to death.

And then if that is not bad enough. While Job is standing at the grave side of his ten children...mourning the death of his loved ones and grieving the loss of all that he had ever owned...a terrible disease comes upon him, and his skin becomes infected in such a way that he only can dream of death.

According to the book of Job, here is a summary of his physical ailments:

- Inflamed, ulcerous sores
- Persistent itching
- Degenerative changes in facial skin, disfiguration
- Loss of appetite
- Fears and depression
- Purulent sores that burst open, scab over, crack, and ooze with puss
- Worms that form in the sores themselves
- Difficulty in breathing
- A darkening of the eyelid
- Foul breath
- Loss of weight
- Excruciating, continual pain
- High fever with chills and discoloring of the skin as well as anxiety and diarrhea
- In addition, Job endured delirium, sleeplessness, and the rejection of friends.

All in all, Job became the personification of misery. And remember, this all happened even though Job was a very godly man!!!

There is a myth that exists that godly people do not suffer any type of ailment—whether it be physical, mental, emotional, or even spiritual—but unfortunately that is a lie because Jesus even suffered at Gethsemane when he was about to be crucified.

As a matter of fact, Jesus addressed this myth in the Gospel of Luke, the 13th chapter. In that chapter, Luke recorded the words of Jesus as he challenged the false perception of the Jews. A perception that said, "if you were godly, you did not suffer."

Jesus refers to a group of Galileans who were killed by Pilate and He asks, "Do you think that these Galileans were worse sinners than all the other Galileans, because they suffered in this way?" "Or those eighteen on whom the tower in Siloam fell and killed them: do you think that they were worse offenders than all the others who lived in Jerusalem?"

To both assertions Jesus answers unequivocally—-no!!!

Jesus dispelled the myth of if you are a good Christian...you will not suffer.

Job, a godly man, an upright man was suffering and this suffering pushed him to the brink of his ability to cope and yet even though his story turned out redeemed and great...I still get aggravated thinking about it and want to push God off the throne and replace him with my brilliant mind, because let's face it, "Couldn't we all do it better?"

Years ago, I read a book entitled, "The Shack" and that book messed me up. There was a part of the book where the main character got to sit on the judgment seat of God and at that moment, I realized that I would not know what to do. If I killed someone who deserved, it in our world would that really make all things better? Could I explain everything, heal everyone? Do I even have a clue as to what all is really going on?

I do not know. What I do know is that I simply need to press into Jesus when times are bad and that, unfortunately, is the best I can do at times. But it is enough. I cling to Him because in Him lies hope. In the midst of "The Shack's" discussion about suffering a quote is given which I cling to.

"Grace doesn't depend on suffering to exist, but where there is suffering you will find grace in many facets and colors."

As we move forward through this world here is hoping that you cling to Him and allow His grace to flow freely in your life...no matter what life may bring. That grace will then serve as a catalyst for healing. As His grace flows in us and through us it transforms us even though we will still have many unanswered questions. It is part of the process, but it does make a difference.

<u>Human Trafficking Statistics and What You Can Do.</u>

The (trafficking victim protection act) TVPA, as amended, defines sex trafficking as "the recruitment, harboring, transportation, provision, obtaining, patronizing, or soliciting of a person for the purpose of commercial sex." While adults must be compelled to perform commercial sex by force, fraud, or coercion in order for it to be considered a severe form of trafficking in persons, this is not the case for children. By law, children under the age of 18 who are induced to engage in a commercial sex act are considered victims of sex trafficking. In addition to a minor engaging in a sex act in exchange for money, examples of sex trafficking include a minor engaging in "survival" sex (**i.e., the victim engages in sex in order to obtain basic needs such as food, shelter, or clothing, which are considered something of value**) and participating in certain types of pornography

Trafficking is prevalent everywhere: STATS

<u>STATS:</u>

There are 193 members states as part of the United Nations, only Vatican City and Palestine are not included in our world. Of those, only 13 actively criminalize slavery.

The International Labor Organization in 2017 estimated that HT is a 150-billion-dollar industry. In 2019, The Government Technology and Services Coalition reported that Human Sex Trafficking made 99 billion worldwide.

The ILO also estimated that in 2021 there were 50 million people (about twice the population of Texas) were being held as slaves. The United Nations reported that as of 2023 there were 60 million.

The number one consumer of sexual material and slaves, according to the US Dept of STATE TIP report (2012) was the United States. A University of Oklahoma report stated: the US has become the top destination for sex tourism in the world.

The United Nations determined that 1 in 113 around the world are in danger of being trafficked.

However, we really do not know how many people are being trafficked. The group, "California against sexual exploitation" in 2019 determined that only .04% of HT survivors were ever identified.

According to Shared Hope and the US Attorney General's office, 300,000 teenagers are sold for sex in the United States each year and 80% of them are US citizens. 2 children are sold every minute

According to the FBI and Department of Justice, the average lifespan of someone being trafficked is 7 years.

Average age according to the US Dept of Justice is 11 to 14.

Of those who were trafficked for sex, most were molested by family members from the ages of 6 to 10; 30% by family members; 14% by family friends (Counter Trafficking Data Collaborative Global Hub of Statistics). 45% were recruited by family members and another 20% by friends of family members. 20% by an intimate partner.

68% of minors were trafficked while living at home (National Research Council along with National Criminal Justice Reference Service).

National Center for Missing and Exploited Children: 1 in 7 runaways are victims of HT, 1 in 3 are approached within 48 hours. (1.6 to 2.8 million kids/teens run away from home each year, 90% return home but 300,000 end up on the streets and trafficked).

—-

According to the FBI, 60% of kids recovered from sex trafficking were from the Foster Care System. (there are about 500,000 in foster care in the US) New York State reports that it is higher at 75%. (OLP Foundation) Traffickers refer to it as "shark the block" where they wait for girls to walk to the corner store to take advantage of them. In Florida, 29% of teenagers in Foster Care are in Group Homes. In some counties it is as high as 36%. Broward County Public Defender Gordon Weekes His letter to the head of DCF alleged that child-welfare workers knew girls in the group homes were targeted by sex traffickers, "yet little has [been] done to address the traffic recruiter that prowls the area seeking out vulnerable girls in foster care as prey."

"Knowingly placing highly vulnerable foster care girls in such an environment without protection is tantamount to state-sponsored human trafficking, and it must be stopped," Weekes wrote.

There are 249 group homes in Florida. Only 18 are approved to house HT kids. 150 Have HT KIDS, they are only supposed to be in group homes for a max of two weeks by federal law. Office of Program Policy Analysis and Government Accountability found that 21% of the 377 verified child trafficking victims in 2021 were in DCF foster care.

According to Florida records, a child that is identified as an HT kid moves on average 21 times while in the care of DCF. (Univ of Miami report). One child was moved 142 times from ages of 12 to 18.

Professor Reid at USF was blunt in titling a 2018 report "System Failure! Is the Department of Children and Families Facilitating Sex Trafficking of Foster Girls?"

Reid is director of USF's Trafficking in Persons — Risk to Resilience Research Lab. In a relatively small study she conducted, she found that three-fourths of the trafficked foster girls she examined were not exploited until they were placed in Florida's foster system. (one foster care child wrote...)

> ¨being *in foster care was the perfect training for commercial sexual exploitation. I was used to being moved without warning, without any say, not knowing where I was going or whether I was allowed to pack my clothes. After years in foster care, I did not think anyone would want to take care of me unless they were paid. So, when my pimp expected me to make money to support 'the family,' it made sense to me.*

Consider the 11-year-old who's removed from her biological parents after Child Protective Services discovers abuse at home.

She's taken, perhaps in the middle of the night, to an emergency shelter. If no beds are available there, she may spend the night on a cot in a state office building.

She can't stay at the emergency shelter for more than a few weeks. So, she's placed in a long-term shelter, or maybe a group home with several other children. If she has younger siblings, she might be separated from them, depending on where foster families are available.

Within a matter of weeks, she has encountered several caseworkers whose titles can be difficult to keep straight: the investigator, the family-based safety services specialist, the temporary managing conservatorship worker.

By the time she turns 13, she has shuffled through three or four different placements and several more caseworkers. She begins acting out at school, getting into fights, struggling with depression. Her parents have failed to make the necessary changes to get her back. Her relatives are willing to take in her younger siblings, but they fear she'll be too much work. Now a teenager, she faces a low possibility of adoption. No one, it seems, wants her.

She decides to run. The foster care system sets children up for a series of rejections. More than 1,000 children in long-term foster care ran away between September 2015 and August 2016, the majority teenagers. One in four did not return.

But it is not just foster care that makes someone vulnerable...social media is also a big issue.

Thorn: a 2018 study reported that 55% of domestic sex trafficking survivors met their traffickers for the first time online.

Facebook is the most widely used site to advertise for HT

Government Technology and Services Coalition, Feb 2019. A child is sold and raped in the US every 30 seconds. The average person will return to the life SEVEN times before getting out. 80% have been advertised online.

As a result of the increased online presence since Covid, 1 in 5 children are sexually solicited while online today.

There has been a 200% spike in child sex forums (foreign policy.com site) since pandemic.

But there is also a telling statistic for the church. According to the Barna Research Group, 65% of men are addicted to pornography. 50% of pastors.

<u>Language of the trafficker</u>

- Automatic—girl under pimp control who operates without supervision.
- Bottom—the person in a stable (((define))) who is appointed by the trafficker to manage, recruit, and supervise the other girls.
- Quota—the amount a victim must earn for his/her trafficker each night.
- The Life—term used by victims to describe being involved in prostitution.
- Daddy—the term a male trafficker often requires his victims to call him
- Branded—when a trafficker tattoos a victim to show ownership

- Family/Folks/Stable—term used to describe the environment created by the trafficker, an attempt to recreate the family structure so many lack.
- Renegade—a person involved in prostitution who is operating without a pimp/trafficker.
- Pay for Play—(P4P) paid sex, term often used by buyers
- Circuit, track, runaway and stroll given area associated with prostitution.
- Kiddie stroll—area of prostitution involving victims under the age of 16.
- Lot lizard—at a truck stop.
- Seasoning—the process of preparing a victim for the life. Physical and sexual violence, psychological manipulation and abuse, physical and emotional deprivation, isolation, threats, and intimidation.
- Gorilla pimp—exercises control through violence.
- Turned out—the act of being forced into prostitution.
- Out of Pocket—situation where victim makes eye contact with another exploiter (strictly forbidden) or otherwise shows disrespect to his/her exploiter.
- Pimp Circle—punish a wayward victim.
- Ho line—a communication network used by pimps between states, cities, and regions; used to buy and sell victims.

<u>What a trafficker looks for: vulnerability and how a person gets trafficked</u>
The key for the trafficker is vulnerability. They seek those who are in need of something.

They scan the internet, social media sites, looking for people who are lonely, wanting more in life and frustrated, etc...

When a teen or kid feels misunderstood or emphasizes "no one gets me" the trafficker will say, "I understand you."

- I'm not feeling loved, I am sick of being single, I wish I had someone around for me. "I love you."
- I'm not feeling beautiful, I want you to like my body and think I am desirable. I am so ugly, how do I look? Check out my new pics, what

do you think? "I think your beautiful, I'll encourage you to show your body, use your body."

- My life is not going well, being fulfilled. My life sucks, is this all there is to life? "I'll make your life better."
- I don't have friends/family who care, "I'll be your best friend."
- I want to be treated as an adult, I want my independence, I want to take risks, my parents don't trust me, I am being treated as a kid. "I'll encourage you to take risks, you are an adult, you deserve freedom and independence.
- I am scared, I need to get out of here, someone save me. "I'll protect you."
- I want to be successful; I wish there was a way to make quick money, need to make some real money. "I'll make you successful."
- I'm not confident, I don't know what to do, is this right, I don't know who I am . "Trust in me, I will encourage you."

Remember…the ways people get trafficked are varied:

1. Family members sell children.
2. Violence and force.
3. Seduction.
4. Peer recruitment.
5. Befriending.
6. False advertising for modeling, acting, or dancing opportunities.
7. Internet enticement through chat rooms or profile sharing.
8. Promise of a better life.
9. Survival sex—do it to survive. (over 22% of those who age out of foster care are homeless). Get trapped (Canada border…do it or the police will get called…you are indoctrinated that the police are bad).
10. "I am in love with you" but I need a little help
11. Grooming process is often important.
12. Party…room in Tampa (teacher)
13. In the mall…you should be a model.

<u>So, what can we do?</u>

We must pray.

We must do.

Children and Youth Ministries have to become the priority of the church. We get a chance to plant seeds and all too often it is relegated to whoever we can get to do it. We have to re-orient and re-prioritize in the church.

Get involved in HT awareness. Taskforce groups in the county; non-profits; churches.

Start a ministry.

Keep your eyes open and if you see something say something.

We have to create a culture where it is ok to ask for help. All too often we don't talk about what is going on in the church. If you are suffering, put on that good face. We have to get real. It is ok to get counseling...it is not a lack of faith or demon possession to have issues and struggle.

We can make a difference and it is never too late to do something.

BikersAgainstTrafficking.org

Resources Quoted

Allendar, Dan, *Healing the Wounded Heart* (Grand Rapids, MI: Baker Books, 2016).

Swindoll, Charles, *Job* (Nashville, TN: Harper Christian Resources, 2008).

Yaconelli, Michael, *Messy Spirituality* (Grand Rapids, MI: Zondervan, 2002), 13-15; 47.

Yancey, Philip, *What's So Amazing About Grace?* (Grand Rapid, MI: Zondervan, 2002), 11.

Young, William P., *The Shack* (Thousand Oaks, CA: Windblown Media, 2008).

About the Author

Patrick "Doc" Nave, ABD, DMin., LMHC, MCAP, CTP, Diplomate in Trauma Therapy is a pastor, former missionary, trauma therapist and abolitionist who seeks to partner with individuals on their journey towards hope, healing and renewal. Doc is the Owner of Sojourners Recovery & Wellness Center in Lake Mary, Florida; the Clinical Director of Family4Today; and the International President of BikersAgainstTrafficking.org which has Chapters around the world. Doc loves his Harley Davidson motorcycle; drinking really good coffee; exercising and spending time with his amazing family.

Read more at Family4Today.org.